A LIFE PRESERVER IN A SEA OF DEBT

Wandering Sage Publications is a division of
Wandering Sage Bookstore & More, LLC.

First Edition.

Genre: Self-Help / Financial

ISBN: 9781933300160 – perfect bound 6x9, 255 pgs.
1-933300-16-7

A LIFE PRESERVER IN A SEA OF DEBT

How to acquire a new mindset to transition from overspending to permanent financial stability and have fun doing it

By someone who has accomplished it…

Judy Guralchuk

The most fatal illusion is the
settled point of view. Since
life is growth and motion,
a fixed point of view kills
anybody who has one.

Brooks Atkinson
American Drama Critic
(1894 -1984)

ACKNOWLEDGEMENTS

I'd like to thank my husband for his lifelong commitment to wisely handling money and for teaching me his secrets. Without his expertise, help, and suggestions, this book would not have been written. His patience, understanding, and encouragement saw me through many hurdles along the way.

A special thanks to my son, David, who helped me broaden the spectrum of money saving techniques, worked so diligently on my computer problems, and offered untiring help.

A note of gratitude goes to K. J. Bronson, F.N.P.C., for her input on endorphins.

I am indebted to my son Marc, and daughter-law, Kelly, for all the hours they spent helping me, even though their own schedules were hectic.

I'm grateful to Sigrid Macdonald. As my editor, she understood my shortcomings as a writer, due to my handicap, and went the extra mile to insure the proper intent of my message. I had a story to tell and Sigrid clarified it while keeping with my original objective. She is largely responsible for seeing *A Life Preserver in a Sea of Debt* getting published.

Thanks to Kathy Dunnehoff, Debra Moss, Sharon Randolph, the writers of Authors of the Flathead, Barbara Knutson, Art Asher, Donna Johnson of the Montana Council on Problem Gambling, and Keith Whyte of the National Council on Problem Gambling.

It gives me pleasure knowing this book will help many people begin a better financial lifestyle.

TABLE OF CONTENTS

As a society we begin our adult life already in debt. The average college graduate begins his working career with more than $2,000 in debt.
Is this what our culture demands of us?
Is this a predetermined right of passage we must endure?
As the economy worsens and the average household credit debt increased by 4.8% consumers owe $970 billion or $8,255 per house.
This seems to be a downward spiral from which we can never recover. Becoming financially stable has taken the place of "the pursuit of happiness" in the hunt for "the American dream" of yesteryear.
This monstrous beast seems insurmountable as it accumulates
faster than we can control it…or does it?

MONEY

Respect it

Protect it

It will take care of us

INTRODUCTION

MY TRIUMPHANT EVOLUTION TO FINANCIAL ASTUTENESS

This is my success story of transitioning from debt to financial stability. Let's start at the beginning…

When I was growing up, my parents did not discuss money matters with me. Like so many others, I grew up with little knowledge of financial awareness.

My first marriage was lived in constant financial chaos. We spent more than we earned. We robbed one source to pay another. When this became too complicated, we borrowed money from family. I felt so embarrassed when I had to ask my parents for money because I knew we would never repay them. We tried to refinance our car loan, but were told we owed more money than the car was worth. I wanted to purchase a less expensive car but my husband overruled my suggestion. He was the aggressor and I was non-assertive.

Once we ran out of milk for our daughter and had money to either buy milk or cigarettes. My husband bought cigarettes and I had to borrow from my parents to buy milk.

During the last years of our marriage, I was so sick and tired of my husband's spending that I wanted to fight back. Even though we were in debt, he hired a lawn service, so he could relax on the weekends. He also squandered more on his business charge account than was reimbursed by his company. At that time I was working and trying to save my salary. But he used that money to square his business account. I felt I was working for nothing because we never had anything to show for my hard work.

I had three children to care for, landscaping to be weeded, and a house to keep clean. I had no time to rest. To get even I hired a house cleaning service and began going to the beauty parlor to get my hair done. I deserved relaxation, too. The reality of this situation, of course, was that we were both making a bad situation worse.

Through all of this, I yearned to live within my means and know with a clear mind that if an emergency did arise, it wouldn't put me in the poorhouse. But I did not know how to accomplish this.

Our marriage, like many, consisted of one free spender – my husband – and one worrier – me. Seventeen years of money wars resulted in divorce. At last my money problems were over! "Yippee, now I have total control of my destiny" or so I thought…

It was not easy as a single parent working two jobs, trying to run a household, and paying off huge medical bills. We struggled financially and emotionally. Several years later, when the children were grown, the marital house was sold.

Without understanding that my spending patterns would land me back in debt, I bought everything I wanted for my first apartment: rugs, curtains, furniture, and pictures. When cash ran out I charged, rationalizing that I needed everything *now*, lacking awareness that there was a better way to manage money.

The interest from my divorce settlement paid my rent. In the late 1970s interest rates reached 12% and, unrealistically, I thought it would last forever. The extra money produced a pseudo feeling of being rich and it cried out, "Spend me." And that is what I did.

I worked as a low paying bank receptionist. I wished I could have gotten a better paying job, but they all required typing. Cerebral palsy spasms in my hand, caused by a stroke at birth, prevented me from typing. To supplement my income, I worked extra jobs for nine years. The additional money, again, gave me a false sense of richness. I spent both paychecks. What was I thinking? Such a web of debt, confusion, and stress I wove. One second job was at Macy's Department Store. I ended up paying them more than I made each month to cover my shopping.

Between my two salaries I was earning $16,000 a year.

Interest rates dropped in the 1980s and I had less money coming in. Not only did I have to meet most of my rent out of my paychecks, but I also had to pay off huge credit card bills as well. I paid minimum payments and was drowning in debt. I had managed to screw up my own finances worse than I ever did with the help of my ex-husband.

Then I met John, whom I later married. He had just returned from a vacation in the U.S.S.R. I learned during our ensuing relationship that he had the funds to travel there because of his financial astuteness. Friends and coworkers thought his radical financial and health lifestyle bordered on fanaticism, but he did not view it as such. He said, "I do not want to live like most Americans." He did not want to spend money indiscriminately and go into debt, nor did he want to eat an unhealthy fare. All around him he witnessed others stressed over debt and fall victim to diseases from poor nourishment.

He strived to be different. His feet were firmly planted on the ground; he knew exactly how he wanted to live and what he wanted to accomplish. Nothing could sway him, and I mean nothing! He said, "If you cannot make it here in the United States, you cannot make it anywhere." The reference being that when we handle money astutely, work hard, and maintain our health, we succeed in our endeavors. He did not consider himself a tightwad or a scrooge (sometimes I thought he was), and he did not feel deprived. He viewed himself as financially aware. His lifestyle was the extreme opposite of mine. (But he was eventually responsible for my financial turning point).

John was not a wealthy man, just an average guy trying to get as much as he could with the funds he had. He worked as a lifeguard and then a marine safety officer. John's salary was $26,000 a year.

As time went by I learned how he maintained financial security. He always lived beneath his income and was frugal in all aspects. He was happier to see money saved than spending any more than he had to. John was content with his selected standard of living. He chose to invest in property rather than throw money away on inconsequential purchases. Later, after we married, selling those property investments allowed us to build our home with cash.

While we dated I found myself wishing I had his money smarts after my divorce. What a difference this would have made in my money handling. I would have scrimped to the bone to make my bank salary stretch and enjoyed doing it. Instead of using a portion of the principal of my divorce settlement for purchases I could have deferred, I would have tried to add to the principal. Certainly, I would have saved the salary from my second jobs. At least I'd have had something to show for my hard work.

Before we married, I paid off my debts, and invested what was left of the divorce settlement. But in the first years of our marriage, I found myself resenting John's penny-pinching ways, even though I knew he was right. I felt he pressured me to be as frugal as he was and I wasn't emotionally ready to alter my spending habits. When I explained how I felt, we came to a compromise we both were satisfied with. He would respect my need to have a little spending money and I would try to understand and accept his philosophy on spending, which was to be content saving money, paying less, having less, and consequently, not having debt and chronic stress. I wanted to change, but first I had to let go of the magnet of perplexity that held me back. I found myself wanting to cling to my old ways, to justify what had defined my spending in the past, but at the same time, I wanted desperately to make the transition to live debt-free.

I can't remember exactly what defined my turning point of crossing over from one financial mindset to another, but one day I stomped my foot down in determination, deciding John wasn't going to be the only person in our marriage to live financially astute. I saw tangible results. We saved money every month and also managed to have enough in our checking account to cover all our expenses, including emergencies.

I'd wanted financial security for so long and here it was! I was ready to blend scrounging with inconsequential purchases. I was ready to have a romance with money.

John had thrown me a financial life preserver, which I tightly caught hold of, and will never let go. Using John's economic philosophy as a model, I made observations and suggestions to incorporate into our lives and had fun in the process.

Slowly, my attitude changed toward spending. I acquired self-confidence to reprogram my money awareness. Since we began living in the same financial mode, our ties are stronger. There's no anxiety, resentfulness, or hiding expenditures. We have the same goals. We both benefit. And I love watching our savings grow.

I learned that there are many ways to become a responsible money saver and spender. John knew the differences between spending rationalization and realization, and he taught me these things, as well.

After all the self-inflicting money troubles I caused myself, John appeared to show me the way out. I learned to turn it around and so can you!

John's financial philosophy made it possible for me to accomplish the transition from overspending to a life of financial stability. I call this process positive attitude adjustment. Each chapter shows how to weave it into all walks of life.

This book is for those who wholeheartedly want to overcome great odds to better their economic situation. Even though I take a no-nonsense approach to overspending, I will understand your predicament. I have lived it. We repeat mistakes of our past even knowing we are responsible for our actions. These errors, which caused anxiety, stress, and turmoil, will be replaced with uplifting satisfaction. We will learn John's secrets of attaining financial stability as we reprogram our spending habits.

Money savings ideas are everywhere: in magazines, newspapers, in books, and advertisements. There are articles listing ways to save money, and how to save using cents-off coupons. Entire books have been dedicated to saving money. Credit companies advertise to help us get out of debt. We listen to suggestions, read books, and get money savings information, but still fail at achieving our financial goals. What's been missing is the psychological formula that is necessary to permanently integrate a new savings' mindset. This book will show us how.

I have not received any formal education in psychology. But through experiencing life from two financial extremes for more than forty years, I have been able to recognize my errors, correct them, and move forward.

Scenarios will be used to explain the transitioning process. They come from John's secrets of financial success, my own experiences, encounters with others, and hypothetical situations. We can personalize scenarios by injecting our own life situations.

I believe John's money management techniques will not only help businesses achieve greater financial awareness but will rid our country of all personal indebtedness as we know it today.

So come with me on the last adventure you will need: to once and for all acquire permanent financial stability!

CHAPTER 1

POSITIVE ATTITUDE ADJUSTMENT

PART 1
UNDERSTANDING OUR PRESENT SPENDING HABITS

Before embarking on the road to understanding our spending habits, we need to know the definition of positive attitude adjustment: Acquire a fresh mindset to permanently live debt free. (Past spending practices are replaced with an innovative awareness of buying choices). Positive attitude adjustment (PAA) is our life preserver, which will lead us from drowning in a sea of debt to floating in economic stability.

It offers a financial reawakening to get us to stop overspending, get out of debt, and start saving money.

The positive attitude adjustment process:

1. Identify problem-spending areas and reduce expenditures, thereby having more available income to save and invest.
2. Embrace a willingness to change.
3. Motivate yourself to take action.
4. Think about future goals and dreams. Are they more important than a huge home, designer clothes, having more electronic equipment than the Jones's, or a more expensive vehicle than our neighbor?

5. Make the commitment to abolish financial slavery and achieve economic stability. Be determined and consistent. As we start seeing results, and as a positive attitude becomes habit, debt will no longer be part of our lifestyle.
6. Have fun in the process and never live from paycheck to paycheck again.

Adjusting our attitude requires an optimistic approach. We change old self-destructive spending habits for new constructive ones. At the end of each month we are in control, have money to save and enjoy peace of mind.

Anyone can rationalize the way money is spent. This is a defense mechanism. Yet, it is helpful to keep an open mind, as that will benefit us.

When we have a history of overspending, it's usually a lifelong learned habit that comes so automatically we may not be conscious of it. We need to stop and reevaluate our situation. Sometimes we keep doing things without realizing there is a better way until someone makes us aware. This awareness helps eliminate the quiet desperation within us regarding money issues.

The positive aspects of developing PAA:

1. More confidence and security
2. Self-rewarding: financial stress no longer has a home in our thoughts.
3. An increased thirst for more money saving techniques and willingness to listen to other's ideas
4. Feel exhilaration and enthusiasm as we move towards financial stability
5. Goals are realized

We cannot change our past spending habits but we can learn by our mistakes and diligently want to change for the future. Once we make the decision to transition, we are ready to adopt positive attitude adjustment.

Pinpoint motivations that lead to overspending:

1. Lack of awareness of spending on nonessentials
2. Negative emotional states such as depression, anxiety, boredom, frustration and sadness
3. Positive emotional states such as happiness and causes for celebration
4. Spending for the sake of spending
5. Too much cash in our wallet, giving us a false sense of richness
6. Trying to keep up with the Jones's
7. Peer pressure
8. Not knowing we have choices

Overspending does not cure any of the above. All it does is give us worry, debt, and stress. Using this list and some ideas of our own, we can address the actual reasons why we overspend. Not until we understand our motivation, and acknowledge, deal, and conquer our demons head-on, are we able to adopt PAA and achieve a permanent debt-free life.

As the Introduction stated, my husband John is responsible for my financial transition. We continually exchange stories of ways we save money. For instance, Smart Balance Spread was on sale from $1.99 to two for $3.00. I used a $.75 off coupon and paid $5.25 for four, or $1.31 each. The same day John needed manure for our garden. The nursery price was $38 for a truck full. We went to a local dairy and paid $10.00. We had fun as we saluted each other. Between us, in one day, we saved $30.71.

Adjusting to new financial philosophies takes time. We all have setbacks, but when they occur, we need to realize they are just delays, not disasters. If we have a setback, pick up and continue. Don't stop. The more new ideas we put to work, the fewer old patterns remain and the more we benefit. After a while, old patterns disappear,

PAA takes over, and becomes second nature. The first attempt at a positive attitude will likely be the hardest to accomplish, but progressively, each new change becomes easier. It worked for me, and it can work for you.

The first step is to change negative thoughts to positive action by modifying spending. The longer we revise, the more innovative ways are incorporated. Conversion may take a long time or a short time. It's our decision. Change our perspective from discontent with the status quo to confidence in the future. Do a happy, zippity hip-hop dance on our toes, throw our hands in the air and shout, "We can do it!"

When masses of people overspend and live constantly in debt long enough, society accepts this as being okay. However, it is not okay. Just because millions fall into this trap, does not mean we need to join them. Stand our ground. Catch the life preserver. Do not allow the actions of others to drown us in a sea of debt.

Eleanor Roosevelt understood this when she said: "When you have decided what you believe, what you feel must be done, have the courage to stand alone and be counted."

Plan financial goals by using these points and ideas:

1. Create a positive environment with those who enjoy money saving strategies. Ignore those who poke fun and make snide remarks. I had a friend who was uncomfortable with my shopping for best prices. I found another friend who enjoys shopping for discounts.
2. Incorporate a positive financial attitude into our normal morning routine. We brush our teeth, get ready for the day, and eat breakfast. Now think of PAA

every morning, too. Let this be our companion throughout the day.

3. Each time we practice positive attitude adjustment; our internal fortitude grows stronger, helping us to reach our goals.
4. If we think we cannot accomplish transition, push just once, then again, and one more time. We will have achieved the impossible and we will thank ourselves for not giving up.
5. It takes but one action or one thought to begin financial fitness. All we need to do is strongly believe that we can do it. Only we put ourselves in overspending mode and only we can change it.
6. Turn rationalization into realization. Destructive rationalization devastates our finances. Realization demands that we be truthful about our financial circumstances, therefore, it allows us to reach our goals.
7. Our attitudes are little things that make big differences.

This scenario will help guide us through the transitional process: I always lived a certain lifestyle, and change was something my mind couldn't comprehend. I got stuck in a rut of habits that I acquired over a lifetime. I moved from childhood into adulthood, gaining good and bad traits from family, friends, and peers. Unknowingly, I took on many of their ideas, some of which involved the way they spent money. After I transitioned I used PAA to increase the good traits and habits of the past and to eliminate others that were detrimental to my goals.

We may wonder why it is necessary to change. After all, what was good enough for family and friends should be good enough for us. Meaning no disrespect to them, I believe that times have changed. We have more modern education, improved consumer products, better communications, and more advanced technologies than ever before, making it possible to improve our attitudes and life in general.

My mother saved money wherever she could, but never on food. That was the unwritten law. I have found that shopping for food bargains is a mainstay for saving money, and it doesn't diminish quality or quantity.

Even though I had been "programmed" not to save on food, PAA made it an avenue for saving. It proves that even the most rigid ideas for one person can be valuable money savers for another. We can personalize any past situation and use it as a money saver, as well.

We need to become aware of these associations to combat our overspending: think of things that our family, friends, and peers did that influenced and molded our way of life. Have we naturally accepted their values, without question, even though at present, they may not be in our best interest?

Making financial plans using PAA:

1. Plan goals for the future. Include money to replace vehicles, go on vacations, buy a snowmobile, save for college, or a new home, boat, or anything else we may wish to save for.
2. Figure out earnings in relationship to reaching our goals. Include all expenditures and savings. This must be done in reality mode. Do we have an emergency account? Some experts say to have three months' salary in savings. Some say six months to a year. Set enough money aside to feel comfortable.

3. Set goals for the most important things on our list. Have enough money set aside to replace an old roof or appliance, or to clean a septic tank. Before PAA we did not think anything about paying monthly installments to buy what we needed. We accepted it as part of the purchasing transaction. Now we know better. This is a perfect instance where we can figure out how much we would have paid in interest and physically put it into savings.
4. Fulfilling our goals should only occur when funds are available. This takes a great deal of planning and PAA. We must decide to withdraw from savings only in dire emergencies; to pay for vacations and Christmas gifts with cash; and to modify our lifestyle by cutting back. Imagine the money saved if every tax refund, bonus, rebate check, and every penny from raises went into savings. The savings from these items alone could pay for insurance premiums, dental emergencies, an expensive vehicle repair, or tide us over in case of a job loss.

Any time we decide to incorporate PAA into our lives is a good time. The Life Cycle chapter explains how children have it easier when they learn early about money management and develop good spending habits that carry over into adulthood.

For adults who haven't had PAA education, it's a different story. In essence, they must start learning it midway through life, when some negative financial habits have been deeply ingrained. A positive attitude is harder to achieve. However, with awareness, fortitude, willpower, and perseverance it can be accomplished. Hunger to spend money will be replaced with hunger to save money and live debt-free.

There are many two-income households. We have more disposable income than ever before and, yet, many of us are in debt. If the income of one family member is suddenly cut off, will there be adequate funds to see the family through the crises? From my past experience of mismanaging finances, I suggest that we save as much of the second income as possible. It not only provides a nest egg cushion, but it also gives us something to show for our hard work.

Saving money every day is helpful for all types of contingencies. Instead of charging or borrowing money for emergencies, we have cash in hand in case we need to attend to storm damages, taking care of an aging family member, or an extended illness.

Everyone who has said, "I wish I had more money for…" would benefit from learning PAA. When we practice PAA, we learn to live within our income, so there would be more money to spend for… EVERYTHING!

One or two frivolous purchases can set the pace for the domino theory. It can push us over the financial edge into debt. For instance when we spend money for holiday decorations (New Year's Day, Valentine's Day, Memorial Day, July 4th, Labor Day, Halloween, Thanksgiving, and Christmas), it puts a dent in our budgets. Choose just a couple of holidays instead of splurging on all of them.

Eating out, using meal delivery services, buying unneeded additions to our wardrobes, going often to movies, renting videos, drinking daily cappuccinos, and purchasing tobacco can domino. Remember, cutting back on, or eliminating any or all of these extras, will benefit us.

When we are aware that one frivolous purchase can result in the snowball effect, we can avoid buying it. But, let's say that we do make an unnecessary purchase. Using PAA, we know to cut back on something else to make up the difference.

Some items are considered comfort needs. We think these purchases will bring us joy but in reality, they bring us stress instead, by increasing debt and diminishing our savings capabilities. Example of comfort purchases:

Espresso: One a day per day costs $3.50
One a day for one month costs $105.00
One a day for one year costs $1,277.50
One a day for 10 years costs $12,775

Cigarettes: One pack a day costs $4.50
One pack a day for a week costs $31.50
One pack a day for a year costs $1,642.50
One pack a day for 10 years costs $16,425

Alcohol Bar Bill: $1,500 a year
$15,000 for 10 years
$500.00 a year for home alcoholic purchases
Total alcoholic purchases for 10 years – $20,000

Video or DVD rentals: Cost per day $3.89
Cost of two a week $7.78
Cost per year at two a week $404.56
Cost for 10 years $4,045

Movies: Cost per ticket $7.75
Cost of two tickets a week $15.50
Cost per year two tickets per week $806.00
Cost for 10 years $8,060 (not including the popcorn!)

Crepes: Ham and cheese or strawberry (Cost per crepe $5.00)
Cost one a week $5.00

Cost per month $20
Cost per year $240
Cost for 10 years $2,400

All the things mentioned above, however small and inconsequential they may seem, add up to thousands of dollars a year. The total amount of money spent on these purchases over a 10-year period is $63,705! In a working environment over forty years, savings top $154,820! What a boost this would be for retirement funds!

Think of long-term goals instead of short-lived satisfactions, which sabotage long-term dreams.

Do not practice PAA once and let it fall by the wayside. Get in the habit of exercising it every time we reach for money.

Debt is not a fact of life. In most cases it is a fact of lifestyle. If we live beneath our means, consistently, we are ready for any contingency. We can, however, through no fault of our own, go through one catastrophe after another in a short interval of time, causing debt. Don't worry or borrow. We can bail ourselves out. Work double jobs. We can do it and we will feel much better all around. Please don't rationalize and say, "I can't work two jobs." Remember, we are practicing PAA. We are leaving old attitudes in the dust. As I said before, I worked double jobs for nine years between my divorce and remarriage. It's hard, but it can be done. We may also consider working two jobs temporarily while getting over financial hurdles.

This may result in spending more time away from home, thereby reducing heating and air conditioning bills, thus freeing up more money to save.

My extra jobs over nine years included being a hospital switchboard operator, a restaurant hostess, and working at Jo-Ann Fabrics and Crafts, Mary Kay cosmetics, and Macy's. Between these jobs, budget allowing, I took college courses at night.

John worked extra jobs when he wanted to invest in properties or to increase his savings. He drove a cab, did lawn maintenance, and lived at an inn, rent free, while he took care of the grounds. He banked his salary. He was a security guard at a marina, and took down an old barn, using the wood to build a house.

There are many more ways to acquire extra money:

1. Have a garage sale or initiate a neighborhood/friends' garage sale.
2. Sell a collection such as stamps, coins, CDs, books, or antiques.
3. Sell our home. Move into a less expensive one.
4. Move from an apartment into a trailer rental or rent a room in a private home.
5. Sell a second home or a vacation cabin.
6. Turn a hobby into a moneymaker by teaching others our specialty skills for a fee, such as carpentry, sewing, woodworking, or quilting. Sell our hobby specialty at a flea market or consignment store.
7. Use money-off coupons to purchase needed items.
8. Rent out a room in our home.
9. Sell unused "biggies," such as old vehicles, appliances, trailers, boats, golf clubs, and musical instruments.
10. Make do with one vehicle.
11. Downsize cell phone plans. Reduce minutes allowed and do not exceed the monthly allotment.
12. Downsize cable TV plans. Why pay for 300 channels when we only watch ten?

When we take the hard road (working an extra job or selling valuables), we highly esteem the sacrifice. It's less likely we will overspend in the future. If we take the easy route and hire a debt consolidator, we are not forced to make important cutbacks, so it is more likely that we will exceed our budget again.

When we opt to earn extra money, it can be used at our discretion: to pay off debt, save for unexpected contingencies, put in a retirement fund, invest in property or stocks, save for a replacement vehicle, or pay for a dream vacation. Think of other ideas to add to this list.

PAA helps plan successful lifestyles as well as financial astuteness. Take education. There are many discipline problems in schools. Time used for discipline takes away from teaching, which is a form of educational suicide. Children should be taught that the more they learn, the more they'll earn as adults. Tomfoolery belongs outside the classroom. The working world shows no empathy for the lackadaisical or the poorly educated. The more knowledge we have, the better the job opportunities. This is reality.

If left unchecked, excessive humor, jokes, and fun, permeate our lifestyles. It's best to frost the cake with these hilarities instead of inflating their importance in schools and places of employment. If practiced in these places, they will definitely result in an inferior education and or a dismissal from work.

Using PAA for financial health leads to ideas for better management of our time, what we eat, where we go, and other aspects of life, as upcoming chapters explain.

When planning future goals, we strive for different dreams. Here are two.

1. We may wish for tons of money so as to live lavishly, or to be involved in sport clubs, parties, social events, and big investments; we might also want to own bigger, newer, and the top-of-the-line boats or vehicles. The list is endless.

Before we know it, this dream can turn into a stressful, complicated nightmare.
2. Or we may fantasize about living a peaceful, contented life, stress free. By practicing PAA, we can do what we know is most important: be debt-free and enjoy life. We can be happy with what we have.

Scenario: Job earnings are $80,000 and spending is $85,000 a year. The stock market plunges, a job is lost, or a serious illness puts us in financial straits. We finally snag a $45,000 a year job. We cannot make ends meet. Our lifestyle is going down the drain. We do not know of any other way to live. Had we known PAA, we would not have spent more than we earned, we would have been able to ease into a lower bracket of living, had the funds to see us through, and had fun while meeting the challenge.

Why is it prevalent that the aftereffect of earning more money results in more money spent? In my past and with others I have known, upping our living scale was an automatic response to an increase in income. We enjoyed our newfound spending power.

But, as we transition, we realize that increasing our plane of living when our income increases is counter-productive to financial stability.

There are others who earn $30,000 a year and save $4,000. These same people could earn $80,000 and save $40,000! And they'd be content and satisfied. When John earned $26,000 a year, he saved over $8,000.

How do we know how much is enough to save? John and I live below our means and buy only what is necessary. When we do buy something, first we compare prices from three or more sources, and then we come to a decision to purchase it at the lowest price, without jeopardizing quality. Our only fixed monthly bills are cable and computer. We have no mortgage, cell phone, or other fixed expenses. We do not spend money on recreation, movies, junk food, or video rentals. I attend a playhouse once a summer. We eat out twice a year. We do not buy clothes unless we urgently need something. We rarely entertain. John has an organic garden and grows much of our year's supply of vegetables and fruits, which I can or freeze. He hunts each year and we eat wild game, only buying poultry and fish, on sale, in supermarkets. We are water drinkers and do not purchase soda, fruit drinks, or alcoholic beverages. We do not grab a bite of lunch in a restaurant when we go into town: instead we buy bananas or apples or take lunch from home. We never buy expensive gifts. This is how we live. We are content, happy, and debt-free.

We do not have a set amount to save each month, but we always have money to save. So whatever we have left at the end of the month automatically gets saved. We save enough to purchase a replacement vehicle when necessary, to replace our roof, pay for any emergencies, big dental bills, vacations, taxes and insurance, etc. Sometimes we save over a third of our income, sometimes less. But when we need to pay for big expenses, we pay cash. We never buy anything on time or pay interest. We do not need to follow a budget because our lifestyle makes it possible to have money to pay all our bills and anything else we need. (More about budgets evolving into un-budgets by practicing PAA in the Un-budget Chapter.)

Everyone's life style is different. What's good for John and me might need modification to suit other lifestyles.

Remember: The most successful people are not always the wealthiest, but the most sound money managers. Financial fitness is determined by what we save, not by what we spend.

Take a stand! There are no other options. Have fun. Cut down. Cut back. Buy less. Live beneath our means. Be satisfied with choices. It's benefiting *us*. Reduce, reuse, and recycle. Find a happy spending medium. With PAA, this can be accomplished.

Scenario: Our TV goes belly up at the same time our vehicle needs repairs, plus an insurance premium is due. What to do? Leave the TV. Pay the vehicle repair and insurance first. Anyone can live without TV. Read, engage in hobbies, go hiking, write an old-fashioned letter, or play a game. Carpool until funds are available to repair the vehicle. Check with the insurance company to find out if there is a grace period.

Scenario: A big sports game is being televised in three days. In preparation, we plan to buy several six-packs of beer and call our favorite restaurant to deliver a big taco salad with all the trimmings and a delicious piece of strawberry cheesecake for dessert. However, before the game, a financial emergency arises and medication and doctor bills accrue. What to do? Before PAA, we rationalized that our beer purchase and food delivery were necessities, and we did not worry or care about paying our medical bills.

After transitioning to PAA, realistically, we pay the medical bills and make do with a cheaper beverage: lemonade, iced tea, or hot chocolate. Instead of ordering food delivery, we make Dagwood sandwiches and an absolutely decadent dessert, made from goodies we have in the house, accompanied by our favorite salad. Yes! Decadent desserts *can* be eaten along side salads, and cheaper drinks *can* be enjoyed! Until now, beer, tacos, cheesecake, and ballgames were sacred. Now, we giggle, realizing we won't die if we modify our ballgame menu. We are not angry and we do not feel deprived. We relax debt-free. We have learned to put priorities into perspective.

Being non-assertive with others, who wish to spend more money than we want to spend, can be injurious to our finances. Assert our views for not joining them for future gatherings. Do not allow us to be pulled in. If they truly care, they will understand and in the future, plans will take everyone's financial status into consideration. And others will feel relieved, as well.

Before PAA: We allowed our lifestyles to drown us in a sea of debt. As we grab positive attitude's life preserver of new spending awareness, our strain and worry gives way to security and peace of mind.

Scenario: Before PAA. Tippyea is an antiques buff. His home is stuffed with antiques from all over the world. He attends every antique show, feeling exhilarated, buying everything he wants, and that is a lot. He rationalizes that he can sell them for a profit, but his expenditures are in the thousands of dollars. He is never able to show the size profit needed to offset the cost. His continued purchasing adds to his debt.

After PAA: Tippyea is still an antiques buff and it's like an illness. He wants them all but his thinking process has changed. He displays calmness and uses PAA skills to guide his purchases. His home is no longer cluttered with debt-inducing merchandise. He now considers an array of realistic choices and acts accordingly, buying only a few at a time that he knows he can sell for a profit.

This scenario plays out in an array of other possibilities: Buying old beat up trucks and refurbishing them, but not having enough potential buyers to show a profit, or making hundreds of birdhouses to sell at fairs, but having larger investments of materials than profits received. PAA suggests that any of these activities or hobbies is fine, but when we depend on profits to justify investments, we need to know the market is large enough to make it worth our while.

How do we know how to recognize the fine line between how much to invest, how much to spend and how much to save? Before spending money for any project or investment, figure out if our finances can sustain the outlay. Research other similar projects in our area in terms of profitability, and if the population is large enough to support our endeavors.

John does not recommend becoming a savings fanatic. We all need to have a little fun, to do what we most enjoy. But first, we need to figure out what the definition of fun is, and only act on that particular thing. Before splurging, we need to make sure our bills are paid on time, in full. Also, assure that not too many things fall into the fun category, or we will be defeating our goals.

Scenario: There are times when we are faced with multiple important expenditures: replacing an old computer, buying gifts, repairs, illness, a root canal, job loss, new appliances, repainting our home, new clothes, vacation, etc. Our old way of thinking permitted us to rationalize that we needed all these things *now*. We charged everything that we didn't have the cash to pay for. We again rationalized that we could get our bills caught up the following month, but the next month came and, still the credit card bill could not be paid in full. Interest accrued. We needed something else, so we charged it, and the cycle of debt continued.

Instead of buying all the "important" things at once, buy the most urgent thing, pay for it, then buy the next most "important" thing, pay for it, etc. No charge, no debt.

After PAA takes over, this scenario wouldn't have occurred in the first place. We have learned that the marketing strategies that used to have us programmed to buy everything that we needed *now*, don't work on us anymore. (More on the great American marketing machine in the Advertisements and Commercials Chapter.)

PAA teaches us to *never* withdraw from savings to pay off credit card or other debt. After debts are paid off, by working an extra job and cutting back to the bone, be certain only to charge or spend what we are able to pay in full each month.

My scenario: During my single years, I had a friend whose closets were bulging with clothes. I admired and wanted to emulate her. I thought she'd like me more. I began filling my closets as well. (This scenario could be applied to other items like, tools, fishing poles or accessories.) The rude awakening came when I realized my friend had the money to do this, but I went into debt because I did it. All of us make mistakes. (PAA could have played the star role in this performance!)

Scenario: Rose-R-Rambo and R-Car-Bushki have three small children. They move into a new home. R-Car-Bushki works while Rose-R-Rambo is a stay-at-home mom. They want to fence in the yard, buy storm shutters, and put in a pool. When Rose-R-Rambo wants something, she always finds a way. Nothing will stop her. She begins to earn money working on the Internet at night when the kids are asleep. Granted, the desired things won't appear magically overnight, but they will come about as the monies are earned.

We had guests looking at our dining room centerpiece of good quality plastic fruits. "Isn't wood better?" they asked. Their rudeness didn't intimidate us at all; it didn't look bad, and even if it did, we like the old-fashioned look. We certainly would not go out and purchase something different just because somebody made a disparaging remark.

Scenario: Before PAA. Tondalaya and Sed Salumbo believe finances should be kept secret from children. They unknowingly let their kids grow up in a fantasy environment. So the cycle begins. The children don't have a clue about financial fitness.

The family vacations on money not yet earned. They don't think about affording the vacation. They want to have fun. Car expenses, meals, motel, and souvenirs are charged.

They are confident that this is okay because they are not aware that they have choices.

The Salumbo family is still paying off the vacation with monthly payments plus interest when school begins. School clothes and supplies are charged. This is the norm for them. This is how it's always been. Then comes a monstrous vehicle repair and Christmas is just around the corner. Their credit card balances are bulging, so they start using another card to purchase gifts, clothes, and entertainment "necessities." The family rationalizes they "needed" the vacation. They didn't want to disappoint the children, Itzy and Klatz. Neither did they want to disappoint them by omitting school purchases or Christmas gifts. They "need" to buy the children at least as many gifts as their friends. (What the children really need is a financially secure home.) They don't realize they are putting the whole family's future in jeopardy. They are teaching the children to overspend, to live for today: self-satisfaction *now*, without a care for tomorrow. But they are not aware that their actions are teaching this.

Shortly after the holidays, Tondalaya is laid off. Only then does the realization of past financial rationalizations come home to haunt the couple. They may lose everything they have. Sed's salary could be garnished or they may even have to file for bankruptcy. They blame circumstances for their plight, but never themselves, even when reality says it was their chosen lifestyle that wove the tangled web of financial ruination. The entire family must pay the consequences.

The Salumbo family after PAA: The family plays simple money games every once in a while with the children. As the children grow, the games advance. Itzy and Klatz learn financial pros and cons before they are old enough to rebel. They learn the value of money, how to be content with what they have and feel secure. (More information on teaching children financial fundamentals is located in the Life Cycle Chapter.)

Tondalaya and Sed save for a vacation. They plan the trip around funds available. They camp out, purchase food from grocery stores, cook over a wood fire, with the children participating and having the time of their lives. Fun has no end. They explore, hike, see deer, chipmunks, rabbits and squirrels in the wild, go on a canoe ride, pick wild raspberries, jump in the lake while holding on to a long rope, and the kids meet other children to laugh with. The vacation continues to incorporate all the things that the family set out to see and each child is allowed to buy one souvenir. The holiday is not only enjoyable, but it also teaches Itzy and Klatz frugality. They learn if a $10 museum entrance fee is required, a more economical place should be found.

On the souvenir subject, have we ever seen a house full of souvenirs from all over the world, displayed prominently in every room? No. After awhile, when the specialness wears off, they are relegated to storage or thrown in the garbage. So, why waste money in the first place? One or two souvenirs would suffice for an evening of reminiscing.

When school begins, Itzy and Klatz have what they need. They do not have more than is needed. There is no vacation credit card debt. There's disposable income available to pay cash, and what credit card balances there are get paid in full, monthly. Tondalaya and Sed are able to save regularly and they have also started a college account for the children.

The Salumbo family experiences a vehicle repair near the holidays. They pay cash without worry. They had not lived beyond their means. Mind you, they don't advertise their personal financial lifestyle. However, since they are good role models, their children know what to expect and are thankful for the family, not just for the number of Christmas gifts they receive.

At Christmas, there are several gifts for everyone. Each person gets what was most important that fits into the budget. A deposit was made to the savings account. Post-holiday credit card debt is non-existent. These are the benefits of positive attitude adjustment.

Shortly after the holidays, Tondalaya loses her job, but she and Sed are secure knowing the money saved, with no debt, will tie them over until she finds another job.

What is the commonality for the following two scenarios and what links do they have to saving money?

Scenario #1: There's a road along a beautiful country lake surrounded by mountains where John and I love to take walks. In the middle of the road there's a small metal survey marker that is just the right size to trip over. I learned to skirt the obstruction, to walk around it, so I do not get hurt.

Scenario #2: I was born with a physical and mental disability. I learned to hide the physical part to avoid ridicule. In private, I strived to do what I could, but in public, I cringed, feeling depressed and inadequate. With John's understanding and support, I have overcome the weights that held me back for so many years.

Having a disability caused me to fight doubly hard to succeed in every endeavor. People without disabilities have it easier, but they still must fight for financial freedom if they have not learned how to do so. Even with PAA, it takes courage and time to change attitudes of the past.

One of the primary objectives for a financially secure future is to stay clear of anything that hampers or hurts our goal. If we need to fight every day to reach our goals, then do it, just as I fight my disability every day. And when an obstacle does get in our way, skirt it. Go around it. Give us a chance. We can do it!

In all out catastrophes such as hurricanes, tornados, earthquakes, or accidents, where we lose all our tangible assets, the world is not going to stop. It may seem to stop, but it does not. And neither should we. Likewise, when severe financial difficulties occur, despite our best efforts, our economic world may still implode, as would anyone's in a crisis situation, potentially leading to a total breakdown of our ability to provide for our family and ourselves. It may be difficult to have an optimistic approach to this scenario. We may have suffered tremendous personal and financial losses, but with the help of positive attitude adjustment we can muster our inner strength to forge ahead and put our life back on track.

POSITIVE ATTITUDE ADJUSTMENT

PART 2
SELF-ENTITLEMENTS

The definition of self-entitlement: Instant gratification: the belief that we can justify any purchase, regardless of our ability to pay. It is an emotional cancer that rots financial security from within.

I am including this special section because this notion played such a big part in my first marriage and contributed significantly to our living beyond our means.

Self-entitlements endanger economic stability by putting a drain on finances. Some of the following mindsets may be holding us back from reaching our goals. Some of these obstacles I was aware of during my first marriage; others did not occur to me until years later.

1. An exaggerated sense of importance, right or wrong. Aggression of ideas, actions, and spending, feeling of

superiority, and preoccupation with self-importance.

2. Self-righteousness: Anyone who dares to voice a different opinion is wrong. They are humiliated and belittled.
3. Pride and stubbornness lock us in to the status quo

These characteristics destroy financial fitness programs. We need to drown these destructive attitudes and allow new breath of reasoning to surface.

Detrimental self-entitlement attitudes that I have heard throughout my life:

1. "I can't worry about 30 years down the road. I feel great now. Anyway, I might be dead by then."
2. "What are ya, crazy? I know what's right. You don't know what you're talking about."
3. "Don't worry. It's only money. It's not a problem."
4. "I'm gonna buy that and no one is gonna tell me not to."
5. "The world owes me."
6. "How dare you question me on how I spend money? I know what I'm doing."

By giving up the self-entitlement disposition, we won't lose a thing. We will gain by having money available to save and to live debt-free.

Scenario: Tiddal, a husband, unknowingly, acted like a big shot by grabbing restaurant checks and showering his spouse with expensive gifts. He said to a concerned parent, "Don't worry about it," all the while trying to impress whoever was close by. He ordered foods to go without a thought and entertained lavishly. He owned expensive cars and was several months late with the mortgage and maintenance payments.

When Tiddal sold his condo, he had to go into a rental because after he paid his debts, there was nothing left for a down payment on another home. Flippantly, he shrugged his shoulders and rationalized in front of others that he chose to rent instead of buying another condo or home. If anyone dared him to tell the truth, he demeaned that person on the spot. "How dare you question my choice?"

Was he was trying to impress others with a pseudo bottomless money-wallet? He was acting like a big spender without a care in the world. Actually, other people didn't care what he spent his money on. They didn't pay his bills. If others knew Tiddal's real financial situation, they'd have thought he was irresponsible. By being macho ("look how important I am, I have so much"), the only person he hurt was himself and those he held dear. He was ruining his family's entire financial stability.

Repercussions of self-entitlement overspending permeate our entire life; they affect marriage, friendships, children (perhaps for years to come), work, coworkers, and health. Out of frustration, our temper flares. We ridicule others to defend our behavior. Is this attitude worth destroying our life?

Tondalaya and Sed Salumbo's scenario in the first part of this chapter is an excellent example of self-entitlement.

My past experience tells me people with self-entitlement attitudes are not open to improving their money-management techniques. But, if they do decide to change, they will benefit.

We should not be so preoccupied with self–entitlements as to diminish our fiscal responsibilities.

Let us think back to all the self-entitlement purchases we made throughout the years. Would that total a college education? Think priorities. Practice PAA. The attitude and lifestyle we live are our choices: We can choose debt, stress, anger, and frustration, or to live simply, being content, while having both savings, and a secure future.

POSITIVE ATTITUDE ADJUSTMENT

PART 3
MAKING THE TRANSITION FROM OVERSPENDING TO A PERMANENT DEBT-FREE LIFESTYLE

As I mentioned in the Introduction, before I met John, my finances were in shambles. When I had unexpected expenses, I ran out of money before payday and promptly, my savings would be raided to cover the amount needed. This scenario illustrates how to achieve transitioning:

John's theory, which he has always lived by, was particularly apparent in April 2006. We had property taxes, homeowners and vehicle insurance to pay, as well as gym dues, prescriptions, and our anniversary dinner. We also wanted to change our electric bulbs to long life, energy efficient halogen bulbs. For the past few months John had started adding to our checking account by spending less in order to increase our balance, so that we would have extra money on hand to cover upcoming bills. By doing this, we were still able to save the same amount of money that we always did; we did not put any less money into savings just because we had big bills.

He decided to wait until May to replace the bulbs and not purchase anything except food, until we got paid again. This example can enhance our understanding of formulating un-budgets. (More about this in the Un-budget Chapter.)

Scenario: Kerchie and Wombley, who have three children, bought a luxury car they could ill afford. It makes him feel like a big man, the leader of the "keeping up with the Jones's" movement. They eat out several times a week, their credit cards are maxed out, and they always spend more than their income. He wonders why they never have enough money for necessities of life or for vacations. He blames everybody but himself. They play round robin with their bill paying and pay the minimum due on credit card debt. The couple is paying enormous amounts in interest. Living expenses are higher than their income. When they make $25,000 a year, they spend $35,000. When they make $35,000, they spend $50,000. They secure loans to pay bills because their motto is "Never use our own money. Borrow to acquire what we need." The results of this behavior are stress, paying exorbitant interest rates, and having no cushion money for emergencies.

Does any part of this scenario hit home? Think of the choices that could have made a difference. When we first begin a life of overspending, it can quickly get out of hand by snowballing into a life of horror!

Think of the consequences of these scenarios and how they affect our family, and our future goals. Make sure they do not happen to us.

With all the ways we can save money, we may think, "My word, every time I want to spend money, I'll feel guilty. That's no way to live." Each one of us needs to put our priorities in order. Then, when we want to buy something, we can do it with a clear conscience. We may wish to eliminate or modify going to the movies, eating out, going on expensive trips or buying designer clothes. Cutting back benefits us. When there's a special occasion, we can go out and enjoy it without money worries. It's our choice.

Don't assume that living beneath our means will lead to psychological turmoil. Instead, think of it as a happy revelation, something that puts us closer to our financial goals. Say goodbye to pessimism. Say hello to paid bills and money left over!

Saving is not a personal sacrifice. It's a way to reach our goals. Feel privileged to have this option. Think of it as an honor.

Televisions are for entertainment. Purses are for holding personal items. Watches are for telling time. Homes are shelters. Vehicles take us to our destinations. Clothes are body coverings. No matter what the price tag on televisions, purses, watches, homes, vehicles, or clothes, they still give the same services.

Hey! We have survived our whole life without the newest gizmo on the market. So why spend money on one now?

Do not just utter the rhetoric of PAA. Have it come from our inner self.

The more sanctimonious our behavior, and the more we rationalize, the longer it will take us to level off our spending and begin saving. I know. I've lived it.

Use self-discipline to rethink priorities. Try it once. Get our feet wet. Go back and do it again until we are comfortable with the new concept. We don't have to define our turning point. We can do it as slowly or as quickly as is comfortable. Do not get overwhelmed. Take it one step at a time. If we fervently want a debt-free lifestyle, we and no one else can make it happen.

If there's an inner force inside us, holding us back from trying PAA, be honest. Find out what the forces are. Confront them. Understand them. Think of ways to overcome them. Then act on them. An inner force can be tossed away as easily as old spending habits. Okay, maybe not so easily or in all situations, but try. I did it and other scenario couples did it. And so can you.

Anything controllable can be changed: How much money to spend, save, and invest, the cost of electric and utility bills and how expensive our vehicles are, etc. Taking advantage of controllable modes, we have opportunities to cut back. This is the time we can easily have excess money to put away for uncontrollable situations.

Uncontrollable conditions cannot be changed: An accident, unexpected repairs, tooth crowns, replacing an appliance, a tax hike, job loss, or disease. The time to prepare for uncontrollable contingencies is when we are in controllable mode. Be prudent, live PAA, save money. Then, if an uncontrollable occurrence rears its ugly head, we will be financially prepared.

When we see something we would love to buy, think, will this purchase interfere with our long-term goals? Can we justify the purchase? Is it a need or a want? Will the one we have suffice?

Scenario: We have extra money in our pocket giving us a false sense of security. We see a product and without hesitation, we buy it. We have committed impulse shopping. Then an unexpected expenditure comes up and we wail, "We never have enough money." After the fact, we realize had we practiced PAA, the purchase price of the impulse item would still be in our pocket to pay for the unexpected expenditure.

When we buy things without thought, purpose, or determining how we can buy it cheaper, we are defeating PAA. If we do blunder, cut back elsewhere so it doesn't put a dent in our budget.

Scenario: Qualapea lives the high life. She has the best of everything, top of the line motor coach, beautiful home, motorcycle, designer clothes, and everything else. Her income has been slashed since the stock market fell. Everything she owns is paid for in monthly installments; even her motor coach will take her 15 years to pay off. It boggles her mind to see John and me living debt-free! She hungers for financial stability but habits of a lifetime stand in her way. In realization mode, she says, "This is my home," referring to the motor coach. "I need the best of everything," (she needs to feel important).

I say it's a rationalization. It's a shelter, transportation, and body drape. If she truly wanted to be debt-free, she could do it. All the expensive tangibles could have been medium priced goods and still have given her pleasure and allowed her to live debt-free.

Know where to spend money wisely: Do we want short-term gratification, stress, and debt, or long-term fulfillment? When we need to buy a high end product, know our needs. Do not buy bigger, better or more expensive to impress others or to feed an inflated ego. It's okay to spend more once in a while, if it fits into budgets, but making it a habit puts goals at risk.

Example scenario shows transition process: Before adopting positive attitude adjustment, Davari, out of boredom, goes shopping at the mall. She falls madly in love with a slinky, shiny black dress that costs $129. She has to have it even though she knows it will put her deeper in credit card debt. Before she has a chance to let this concern prevent her from purchasing it, and with her adrenaline pumping rapidly, she quickly skedaddles to the closest cashier to pay for the dress.

While standing in the checkout line, her heart pounds as guilt and excitement engage in a tug-of-war. She refuses to allow guilt to win. Impatiently, she waits, and then, with clammy hands, pays using her credit card. Needing a pair of shoes to go with her new dress, she meanders to the shoe department and is delighted to find a 9 West slinky black high heel sandal for $69, which she also charges.

Still exuberant, she strolls to the perfume counter where she whiffs exotic aromas from perfume tester bottles. She is so overwhelmed by the magnificent fragrance of Chanel N°5 that she is totally oblivious to the $110 cost as she signs the credit card receipt.

Nonetheless, she senses a captivating element is missing. Realizing that she has no gems for her new outfit, she heads straight for the jewelry department. Visualizing how diamond stud earrings and a necklace, costing $300, would complete her outfit, she charges them, as well. She thinks only of the last purchase amount, rationalizing that as the total amount spent.

She drowns out the cost of the other purchases, as if they were free. All she can think about is how beautiful her tall slim figure will look wearing her new slinky shiny black dress, the matching shoes, the look of the diamond jewelry against her fair skin, and her long blonde wavy hair flowing in the breeze, with Chanel N°5's aroma engulfing her very being.

Excited anticipation prevails but on the journey home, her adrenaline subsides, and is replaced by stress and a nagging sense of dread. Davari will live in fear of having to pay the additional $608 on her credit card bill. She realizes after the fact that she cannot afford such extravagance. But, still these thoughts are not enough to persuade her to return the purchases. Davari is not bored any longer. She is terrified of sinking further into debt.

Here is the same scenario after adopting positive attitude adjustment: Davari, out of boredom, goes shopping for the day, but she tucks PAA in the forefront of her mind. She sees the same slinky black dress. She loves it at first sight. She takes it to the cashier, with doubt running through her mind. While standing in line, positive attitude adjustment wriggles into her consciousness. It asks her, "Do you really need the dress? Can the ones you have suffice? Do you have the cash to pay for it? Do you have accessories for it?"

Thankful for positive attitude adjustments' nudging, Davari realizes she doesn't want the dress, after all. She stops at the perfume counter, feeling the rush of adrenaline, just thinking of all the beautiful aromas and she whiffs a few sampler bottles. This time, as the little voice of positive attitude adjustment returns, it just has to mutter "Ahem".

Davari, smirking with satisfaction, leaves the perfume department and goes home with her money still in her pocket. Davari is a winner today. Her tedium has been replaced with a feeling of exhilaration. She found the willpower to keep her spending in check.

Variations of this scenario:

1. Davari is restless and decides to go shopping. Before leaving home, she decides how much money she can spend without jeopardizing her budget. She takes a list of items that she needs and investigates sale prices. She then goes to discount stores and checks prices. She buys what she needs at the cheapest price and returns home.
2. This time when Davari is bored, she calls her childhood friend Joryann. They pack a picnic lunch, head for the outdoors, and have a fun-filled afternoon munching, hiking, and swimming in the lake. The cost of the outing: transportation.

This concept can be applied to men's suits and aftershave lotions, vehicle accessories, or musical equipment. When we weave our own lifestyle situations into this scenario, we need to end with the same conclusions as Davari's.

CHAPTER RECAP

As we develop and practice PAA, transition occurs.

By eliminating motivations that cause overspending and debt, we look at expenditures in a whole new light. Each dollar not spent brings us closer to our goal.

Setting priorities:

1. PAA first
2. Purchase needed items
3. Wants and splurges only within budgets
4. PAA, traveling at the speed of sound, will slam brakes on impulse shopping
5. Squeezing PAA from our lifestyles is not allowed

Some ideas may seem extreme, but any money management suggestions can be modified to fit individual lifestyles, *if* we don't rationalize. Use PAA at our own pace and be willing to save now, and after reading this book. We must take action as well as wishing to do it.

Positive attitude adjustment is our greatest defense for staying out of debt. It is our helpful "genie" to fall back on, guide us, and help us to realize our financial goals. It checks up on us and appears out of nowhere, if we start to slip. It is our best friend and a life long companion; positive attitude adjustment is our life preserver!

We should not be so preoccupied with self-entitlements, as to diminish our fiscal responsibilities. We are in control of our spending.

As our debts go down and savings go up, our entire attitude changes for the better. One or two slips do not lead to giving up. We get up and start again.

The more we want a debt-free lifestyle the more we will show fortitude in fighting to obtain it. The more we want it, the easier the transition from indebtedness to financial freedom.

As we begin to pay off debt, we do not buy anything more until the debt is paid in full.

A quote from Robert Louis Stevenson, 1850 – 1894, novelist and poet: "There will come a time when we will sit down to the banquet of our consequences." We have choices: living in debt with stress or living debt free with contentment.

PAA increases our quality of life and occurs when we take responsibility for our own spending; it makes money management easy.

Self-gratification expenditures are a thing of the past.

After years of living the PAA lifestyle, I would never go back to my old way of mishandling my finances. This is a permanent way of life for me. I am protected against the financial ravages of bankruptcy, debt, and not having enough money set aside for emergencies and retirement.

This book empowers us all to do the same.

CHAPTER 2

ADVERTISEMENTS AND COMMERCIALS

Advertisers and commercials influence us to purchase their products and ideas and we may not be aware we are being manipulated. Think of all the products we have purchased because we saw them advertised. Would we have bought the same items had we not seen them advertised? How much money could we have saved had we not been influenced to purchase these items? The source of this manipulation comes from the great American marketing machine, which is comprised of corporations, advertisements, commercials and the media.

Advertisers use slick psychology and strategies, including subliminal messages, to convince consumers to purchase their products, whether they are needed or not, whether they are healthy or not, and whether consumers have funds to pay for them. They throw us a line, entice us with their bait, and then they reel us in as their catch. Advertisements have a hold on our spending patterns.

Milton Glaser, author of *Design of Dissent,* says happiness in America is linked to acquisition and owning things. The great American marketing machine devours this quote in an eating frenzy. And consumers do not have a clue that this is going on. We are being manipulated and duped into buying products. Also, we are not aware that these tactics are partially responsible for our debt. We need to refocus what *happiness* means. Positive attitude adjustment's definition of happiness tells us it is more important to be financially secure than it is to equate it with possessions.

Great American marketing machine examples:

1. Charmin®, a toilet tissue company, came out with a dynamic TV commercial, "Please Don't Squeeze the Charmin®." More times than not, whenever I was in the paper goods aisle at the supermarket, I'd see both men and women squeezing the Charmin®. I squeezed it too and indeed it was soft. I bought it, as well as others. This is an example of advertising a worthwhile product.
2. It's two weeks before Easter, 2006. For several seasons, women's styles showed short midriffs, dropped waist pants, and short dresses. All of a sudden the great American marketing machine rises up ubiquitously to advertise style changes that introduce longer tops, natural waist pants and longer dresses. This a convenient time to change styles, both for retailers who benefit by making money from Easter sales, and the clothing manufacturers that make the new styles. They reel in the unsuspecting public, like baiting fish to the hook, knowing we are programmed to buy Easter clothes in the hottest styles every year. After making the transition to live debt-free and understanding how the great American marketing machine manipulates us to enhance their own profits, we can choose not to be reeled in for financial slaughter. What we wore

last year will do just fine. This is an example of being a smart consumer.

3. Yet, we can still be influenced by other advertisement strategies. Companies want us to buy their products *now*. They do not give us time to think about it. The commercial message is to get us all revved up for instant gratification, to experience all the product's promises. They don't want us to hesitate or think rationally. They don't want to lose a sale. This example shows how, through practicing PAA, we now exercise patience before separating ourselves from our money.
4. A television commercial shows a sunny resort with a dozen vacationers decked out with the newest, colorful beach attire. The commercial screams in a loud voice, "You *must* keep up with the newest styles to have fun." Transitioning to financial astuteness says this is not so. What we wear has no bearing on our capacity to enjoy ourselves. Wherever we go, at home or on vacation, we *can* wear what we have. We will not suffer a heart attack or be miserable if we do not buy new clothes. And, this last example unveils still another way to make our evolution to economic astuteness.

This chapter shows how we may have reacted to advertisements in the past and how we need to react to them in the future.

Billboards hit us with bright attention getting colors and script, and promise success if we use their product. Big print and loud colors do not give us a warranty that the product is any better than the one we currently have or that it's superior to others on the market. Billboards are commercial selling engines. However, some billboards are worthy, giving knowledgeable information on community services, travel information and such.

Hypothetically speaking, a billboard shows young attractive people sitting in a brand new convertible, heading toward new horizons. The advertising company would never use older, wrinkled, or heavy-set people. The people in the ads are expensively attired. They are swinging to the sounds of musical notes hanging in the air. They are smiling and having the time of their lives. The message is loud and clear. It's saying, we too can have all this just by purchasing the car. So, we purchase the car. Surprise! It did not give us a new lease on life. We are still living the same life as before. Nor did it come with beautiful people. However, it did come with large monthly payments for the next 4 to 6 years. At this point, we are aware, after the fact, that a good used car would have been the better choice, if we even needed to replace the one we had.

We're taught by big industry, in ads, commercials, newspapers, radio, etc., that we have buying power to purchase whatever it is they're selling. We are a nation of consumption. Yes, we have the ability to consume and possess buying power, but we need to be more prudent. In essence, our buying power makes the seller wealthier, and we, who buy their products, become poorer. People in the ads don't necessarily buy the product. They get paid for appearing in the ad!

Train ourselves not to get all hyped up over ads even though we feel our adrenaline exploding to the stimulus of the advertised product. Use PAA. Keep our cool. Is this particular item absolutely necessary for our survival? (Not in a joking way, but seriously). Do we wish to keep our hard earned money or spend it needlessly?

Television commercials use paid testimonials to convince audiences to purchase the advertised product. Stop. Think. Are these paid people who they are depicted to be, or are they actors, acting out a part?

Ads introduce a wide variety of products and services we were unaware of before. They may give us ideas for the future. We don't have to buy them now just because they're advertised. Tuck the knowledge away for later use.

Magazine ads show young, handsome, lean, and muscular men modeling the newest underwear styles. We may think if we buy some, we too will look and feel like the models. So we buy a few pairs. We find out soon enough that we are the same old us, but out the purchase price. And we may not have needed the underwear at all.

Just as with male ads, beautiful young women are shown modeling everything from A-Z. We may want to emulate them also, but find we are just as we were before buying the advertised item.

Most ads use young models. Very rarely do we see older models selling the newest fashions or the latest underwear. When we do see older models they are selling products geared for senior citizens. The advertising empire is missing out on an important marketing group. There are seniors that have ample incomes and would love to be targeted for the newest fashions and pretty undergarments, the same types of styles currently being advertised for young people.

But most marketing demographic strategies target the younger generation. If we fall into this category, which research tells us spends the most consumer money, we need to be more acutely aware of these tactics if we are to successfully transition.

Flashy ads use psychedelic colors that picture a narrator screaming out excitedly that this is the best, cheapest buy for a limited time only, that we have got to act immediately, that we simply cannot live without the product. The "old us" with adrenaline pumping, and vehicle keys in hand, would have dashed out the door to get there first. The "new us," practicing PAA, would make a sensible note of the product thinking if it was indeed on our list. Then we would include it with other possibilities before actually purchasing it. We may find that it wasn't the best product for us at all.

John and I saw a commercial for a food dehydrator and it offered a special bonus for those who called to order within the hour. We wanted to think about how much we would use it and compare it with other dehydrators before we bought it. We called to order it several weeks later and received the same bonus.

Rule of thumb: No matter how excited we are about a product, investigate other possibilities before buying. This is the way we reprogram our spending habits, using PAA.

We also have found when we call to order an advertised item; the order taker tries to inundate us with numerous other products he is selling. This practice is not for the customer's benefit. The sellers are using us as a captive audience to pitch other products that they don't have to pay to advertise separately. I have actually told an order taker if I have to purchase other items, or listen to their selling spiel, I'll cancel my order. Nothing is worth that kind of pressure tactic. And I won't allow anyone to persuade me to purchase items I did not want in the first place.

Example of media influence to persuade us to buy a product: A swivel/recliner/glider comes with its own ottoman. The sale price is $79.99. The ad shows a football on the ottoman and a bowl of popcorn next to it. The Super Bowl is two weeks away. The football fan in us begins to surface. We feel excited as we think of settling into that soft comfortable chair to watch the game. We envision ourselves holding the football and munching on buttered popcorn while we cheer and scream for our favorite team.

1. With PAA in mind: If we had saved money to buy a similar chair, and it would not jeopardize our budget, then buy it.
2. If we charge it with a credit card that has a running balance, one that is not paid in full each month, do not even consider buying it. Make do with what we have, no matter how enticing the ad.

For relaxation we may choose to watch TV, sometimes for hours every day. We hear commercials in loud, firm, enthusiastic voices telling us we cannot live without such and such product. Have we ever stopped to think loud voices are purposely used to hype us into buying the product? Have we ever once heard a TV commercial spoken in everyday tones? When commercials begin they bellow several octaves louder than the program. Sometimes they are so loud we mute out the whole commercial out of aggravation. Companies who advertise on TV evidently don't think their products will sell if they talk normally. Surprise! At least if they were spoken in normal octaves we wouldn't mute them out.

Advertisements and commercials try to stimulate us though emotional appeal. They use tactics to arouse us into immediate action, never suggesting we think about it first. The guilt game: A children's reading program ad tells parents their children will read better than other children who do not use the reading program. And what criteria would parents have to compare their child's reading with other children? There aren't any. These companies don't care for us personally or care if our children don't need the program. They just want to make a sale. When children need help with reading, many programs are available. With help from school professionals, we can choose the best one.

We need not purchase the advertised reading program out of guilt.

Another example of media influence: A furniture store is liquidating its stock to make room for new merchandise. The TV ad screams out, "No payments for 36 months." "The best markdowns in the history of our company." "Sale ends in eight days." "You must act now." PAA starts to get nervous. First, we already know not to buy anything unless we have the cash and the purchase price does not jeopardize our budget.

If we still want to pursue buying furniture, ask if interest will be charged on the unpaid balance until payments are begun. Secondly, who knows what might transpire in our lives during the 36-month period? The furniture may have worn out, been damaged in a fire or flood, we may move, and it would not fit in our new home, our divorced spouse gets it, or numerous other possibilities. We are then left to pay for furniture we no longer have.

I saw an ad on the Internet several years ago: "How to blow your tax refund." It showed people having the time of their lives, laughing and smiling, along with a list and pictures of irresistible luxuries. Wow! Happy days are here again! The ad implied that buying these things would help the economy. It would reward us for getting a refund and would bring us excitement and happiness. When little PAA saw this, it almost had heart failure. Save tax refunds. That will bring us true pleasure and happiness.

Fight off the long acquired subliminal urges that cause us to overspend. Tread softly. Think about past finances and how we can improve in the future.

Other ads and commercials invoke the opposite of everyday life: feelings such as tranquility, peace of mind and a chance of a lifetime. A travel agency might advertise vacations in exotic places like Three Kings Island in New Zealand, or a canoe trip in the Northwest Territories in Canada. Even though we yearn to go to far-off places, our financial situation may not allow such extravagance. We need to reinforce our will, and recognize the difference between persuasive ads and the reality of our monetary situation. John, by working as a lawn maintenance man as a second job (even though he did not "need" the extra money), was well able to afford a canoe trip from the Northwest Territories in Canada to the Arctic Ocean. He did not go into debt or deplete his savings.

We see commercials advocating throwing away used plastic food containers because they are so inexpensive. They'll assume we will follow their lead, that it's okay to lose them or toss them out and buy new ones. In the first place, the containers must be of a usable quality before selling them and must be worthy of extended use with proper handling. In the second place, every time we repurchase, we put our hard earned money in the manufacturers' pocket. We could just as easily take our repurchase money and physically throw it in the garbage. Think about all the 50 cent or dollar purchases we have used, thrown away, and repurchased. Hands down, the money saved is better in our pocket than somebody else's.

A commercial advertises a new product. We've already read that commercials over stimulate us. The commercial tries to make us feel that our current product is inferior to the newer model. It wants to persuade us not to be content with what we have. It's easy to be drawn into their snare if we don't know there are other options. With PAA we realize our product has the same functions as the newer model. But even if the newer model has an up-to-date function that we would use a lot, would that be reason enough to buy it?

Before purchasing a commercially advertised product, compare prices of similar products from several stores. Only then, an informed decision can be made.

The great American marketing machine wants to program us by repetition to buy, buy, buy. While watching one TV show, we are bombarded multiple times, having to listen to the same irritating commercial. Be on guard. We could hear it so much we could start believing it.

Commercials purposefully leave out vital and complete data, so as to sway our thinking. Have we ever wondered what the small print says on the bottom of the screen during a commercial? What important information is shown for a split second that we have no time to read, which might sway us from buying the product?

Some TV commercials use such irritating voices and show such idiotic nonsense we just want to scream. We may be so turned off by having to view these ads that we vow never to buy the product. However, the advertising company banks on the opposite reaction. The ads are irritating on purpose. The strategy behind these commercials is to ingrain the product into the viewer's mind so when they are shopping, they'll steer toward buying that item.

The media also deluges us with marketing strategies and to the fun syndrome. The state of mind that results from the inundation of images of pleasurable things permeates many areas of our lives. Promotional film posters show actors and actresses having fun smoking. We see commercials where people have fun throwing away everything from cigarette butts to soda cans to papers, all over parks, highways, pristine lakes, and sidewalks. These actions have a negative impact on the public. The public may think that, by seeing these things in ads and films that it is okay to follow suit. However, these actions are not acceptable. Taxpayers foot the bill to clean up these messes. If none of us litters, we would pay fewer taxes.

The fun attitude seeps into every corner of our lives, sometimes keeping us from developing our potential. It may follow us into adulthood, reflecting on our job abilities, where there's usually a higher standard of seriousness. It can even reflect on earning capacity.

This mindset can seep into our spending habits as well. When we are in the midst of the fun syndrome, we tend to say, "Oh, what the heck? It's only money!" and overspending starts to follow us like a dark shadow. We think, "But it was so much fun while doing it," until we see how far it put us into debt.

It's time we took a more serious approach to the feelings we acquire through media ads, films and programs. We need to differentiate between the fun syndrome and the seriousness of our own real lives. We should not co-mingle one with the other. Parents should interact with their children, as well, teaching them to recognize these differences.

Once we understand this concept, we'll be better equipped to avoid going overboard financially.

John is never swayed to buy anything from an advertisement. If the product had been on his list to begin with, he would research other like products first, and choose the most cost-effective.

Newspapers have ad inserts that include weekly sales from discount stores, department stores, pharmacies, office supply companies, hardware stores, to supermarkets. I used to leaf through them all, noting things I would like to buy, whether I needed them or not, and then I would go shopping to buy everything on the list. After adopting PAA, first I make a list of needed items, and then I leaf through the ads to find where I can get the lowest price.

Pharmaceutical companies have taken over television prime time spots to advertise new prescription medications. It's a billion dollar marketing ploy. (I call this the great American prescription drug con job.) Before pharmaceutical companies began advertising new pills, what did we do when we got sick? We visited our doctor, told him/her our symptoms, got diagnosed, and filled a prescription to get better. The point is, doctors prescribe what's best for each patient and they are kept informed of the latest medications on the market.

It's true, we can suggest a new medication we have seen advertised to our doctor, but still the doctor knows what is best. It is possible, when we see new medication advertisements, we may think we have symptoms that they would cure. Ask ourselves, if we had not seen the advertisement, would we still have visited our doctor with symptoms that required the medication? Money savings in this scenario are limitless.

CHAPTER RECAP

1. Ads and commercials have positive and negative influences in our lifestyles. Using positive attitude adjustment, we can discern hype from reality, make wise purchasing decisions, and stay debt-free.
2. Before purchasing any advertised product, compare it to others on the market. Be sure you need it.
3. Beware of the advertising strategies of the great American marketing machine. Its influences are everywhere.

CHAPTER 3

CREDIT CARDS

"Oh, no… Do we really need to bring up this subject?" Why, of course, we do. "Just go away, ppllleeeaasssee!" Are we hiding our faces with our hands in sheer agony? News flash: Credit cards are not going away and neither am I.

Let's begin by finding out what the estimated average credit card balance per household is in the USA. As of August 7, 2008, the Federal Reserve Consumer Credit Report figures show $8,255. And the Commerce Department's 2001 figures shows Americans paid in excess of $50 billion dollars in finance charges. I think this is an outrage. This insanity has got to stop! Interest paid over a lifetime could finance our retirement years, pay for grandiose vacations, or a summer home.

Credit cards make overspending easy because it's almost impossible to keep a monthly running tab on charges.

If we weren't fortunate enough to have parents teach us prudent use of credit cards when we were young, this chapter will help, especially, since we are adopting positive attitude adjustment.

Some adults, however, on their own initiative, have figured out how to wisely handle credit cards. This chapter is for those who have yet to learn the secrets, as well as those who have. It will further enlighten and reinforce good judgment.

Let's hypothesize that an additional credit card will only be used for emergencies. Our other cards are close to the limit. Then we see a spectacular sale item we just can't live without. We con ourselves into saying, "This one purchase definitely falls into the emergency category," leading the way to abusing this credit card as well as the others. Our spending habits of the past are fighting for supremacy.

Whoa! Stop! Think! Who are we going to let win? Will we allow our past habits to win or the desire to regain financial stability? News flash: No one ever died restraining from spending money. We may think we will - the feeling is so strong - but in reality, we won't. Of course, I am not advocating that we disregard medical supplies and life saving equipment, which are emergency expenditures. And, of course, we have the extra money for these things because we have been practicing PAA.

I keep a piece of paper folded around my personal credit card, secured with a rubber band. Every time I use the card, I write down the amount charged. Before I reach the maximum charges I've set, *I STOP.* It's always wiser to stop way below the maximum to have an emergency leeway.

John taught me, through PAA, how to pay credit cards bills in full each month. When our bill comes in, we pay it immediately. Since we have the funds on hand, we do not need to wait until payday. We only use our card for gas, phone orders, and airline tickets. Everything else we pay by check or cash. If we don't have the funds to cover a purchase, we don't buy it.

The longer we pay our credit card accounts in full each month the higher the limit our company *blesses* us with. These companies think they can outsmart us. They want us to feel richer, so we'll charge more, which makes them wealthier, because we end up paying monthly installments with interest. But, no, we do not fall prey to this marketing strategy. Remember, just because our limits rise, our needs and our income do not automatically rise. We still use our credit cards as before and only when needed, not because the company allows us to.

A department store where I have a credit card offers special discounts throughout the year, if I use their card for purchases. They advertise exclusive shopping days, bigger savings coupons, 15% off all-day shopping sprees, and they call it a 'rewards' credit card. The only sure thing about this is that it is a marketing gimmick to reward the store for getting more of our money. Sale or no sale; be aware of marketing strategies that are designed to make us spend more money than we set out to spend.

Before deciding which credit card we need, do research:

1. What is the yearly percentage rate?
2. Is there a cutoff date that we can pay the full balance without being charged interest?
3. Are there annual fees?
4. If our payment is late, will the interest rate go up? How much? If a mortgage or vehicle payment is paid late, even though it has nothing to do with our credit card account, will that also increase our interest rate?
5. Are there charges for cash advances, going over our limit, late payments, and balance transfers? Will going over the limit one time put our credit standing in jeopardy?
6. How are the finance charges calculated?
7. Ask if the company can change any of the agreement terms without notifying us.

8. Credit card companies are notorious for offering low introductory interest rates. Ask how long the low rate will be in effect and what the rate will be thereafter.

Scenario: We are in our 20s, just going out on our own, and we receive an unsolicited credit card in the mail from company "A." Wow! This is great! We apply for another one from company "B." Before we know it, we have incoming cards from company "C" and "D." Each company somehow knows our income and takes it for granted we are responsible for payments. What the companies don't know is how many other cards we have. When we use the available credit on more than one card, it weakens our ability to pay balances in full.

This endangers our credit rating and increases our stress level. It leads to bankruptcy, late payment charges and robbing Peter to pay Paul. Bad credit ratings stay with us for years. When we need a loan, interest rates are higher because we are a high risk.

When we begin to charge with our new credit cards, we don't think of these things. We get excited about charging on all our credit cards. Instant gratification oozes into our subconscious thoughts. We see it. We want it. We charge it. We say "What the heck? It's only a little here and there. It's only money. So what? It's the normal thing. Everybody does it." Before we know it, reality sets in; multiple bills from all the credit card companies squeeze into our mailbox. Then it starts: minimum monthly payments and maximum interest payments. Boy! These credit card companies sure do love us! They're taking all our hard earned money and going on fancy vacations with the interest we pay!

Stop! Do not fall prey to this common scenario. Let's begin again.

So… we are on our own for the first time. We need "a" credit card. We shop around for *one* that will meet our needs. If others come in the mail, we call the 1-800 customer service phone number and tell them we are not interested. Tear the card up or send it back to them. We are in control. We benefit. Remember, anything for sale is for the seller's profit, unless we really need it. And it's our choice to make someone else richer or succeed at financial fitness.

By continuing with positive attitude adjustment, our prudent use of credit cards becomes second nature. When presented with expenditures, we think about wants versus needs. Is it urgent, important, and is what we already have suitable?

We realize the dangers of multiple credit card abuse, therefore, we decide to have only one, and keep track of weekly and monthly charges. We may wish to have two cards, if we are in business: one for personal use, and one for work. We are equally prudent with each card.

Ads tell us credit card debt is okay, and that we are not alone. We can get the help we need to pay our debt from credit management companies. First, credit card debt is not okay. Second, credit management companies are in business to make money. They charge for their services, positive attitude adjustment gets a stomachache, and we plummet further into the sea of debt.

We can pull ourselves up from the drowning waters by catching hold of the life preserver. Add all of the "*it's only 99 cents, $1.50 or $5.99*" purchases for a month. The next month add them again, but do not purchase them, applying that amount toward our credit card debt.

Another way to receive credit card debt help is through AARP's manual, *10 Steps to a Better Financial Future.* It suggests contacting The National Foundation for Credit Counseling at 1-800-388-2227. They offer counseling at no cost, or for a nominal fee, on money management and confidential budgeting, as well as debt and credit card repayment plans. PAA gives a sigh of relief. Also, a non-profit community service organization, Consumer Credit Counseling Service of (your state), offers no fee initial counseling plus other services. Look them up on the Internet.

Scenario: Suddenly we need several items. We are aware that purchasing them all at once will put our credit card balance higher than we planned. Evaluate each item. Figure out the most important one and get that. The following month get the second most important thing. Pay each month's balance in full. Never spend money that has not been earned. We would be surprised how needs can be relegated from number one in importance to further back on the list, or even be categorized as a want.

Our card company is shrewd. On October 15th, 2005, we received an amendment to our contract. At the same time they raised our limit astronomically, they sent us blank checks we could use, charging the credit card. They offered zero interest rates, no fees on cash advances or ATM withdrawals. We can have all these things through the following five-month period, which happens to include the holiday season. The *old* me would have fallen into their web and gone out and wildly charged up a storm. Think of all the fun. I would have felt like a millionaire. But, now, since adopting PAA, their offer didn't entice me. Credit card companies will do anything to put us in debt. I shredded the blank checks. We all need PAA strength to forge ahead and stay on financial track.

Scenario: Rose-Ambo and Are-Kar-Bushki have accumulated credit card debt. They love to travel. They use cards to pay for vacations and all other purchases. They have several children. They love to shower their kids with the best and newest things on the market, regardless of cost. They have two vehicles, two insurance premiums, two registrations and maintenance payments and a large mortgage. Together, they bring home a decent income. They charge because they use ready cash to cover their mortgage, insurance, utilities, and car payments. They wonder why they never have enough to make ends meet. When someone tries to show them how to make changes, they look incredulous. How dare you insinuate that we spend too much on our children, our vehicles, and our home? We need them. The children need them. PAA screams, "EEK!"

Stop. Play back our rationalizations. What the children need most of all are parents as role models, teaching good financial strategies, so there will be college funds and emergency money available if needed. Parents need to realize that showering children with everything does not guarantee them a happy, successful life. PAA benefits us by being open to reeducating ourselves to a more sound financial future.

Scenario: Being raised in this country of plenty — seeing people buying bags full of merchandise to the easy availability of credit cards, to having a friend at the credit card management company — we tend to imitate the masses. It's called going along with the crowd (without even being aware of our actions). It's become a habit over the years. It's catchy. We don't give it a second thought. However, after learning PAA, we reconsider.

Credit card debt has become an epidemic. When we use positive attitude adjustment we rid ourselves of this strangulating illness.

Scenario: To reduce his credit card debt, caused mainly by caring for his parents, our friend Art Asher gives these helpful hints: Pay more each month than charges and interest combined, pay as much over the minimum as possible, pay more on the accounts that charge the higher interest rates, ask credit card companies to lower our interest rates, and pay as soon as the bill is received.

In conclusion, think of credit cards as a privilege, not something we are entitled to. Have a planned usage program before purchasing anything. By utilizing this chapter's information, we avoid the dangers and pitfalls of abusing credit cards. All the scenarios can be personalized to our lifestyle and situations. Remember, credit cards sell debt. And, before reaching for our credit card, have a private conversation with PAA.

If we do not make our stand, we are collaborating with our status quo, our credit card debt, and the American marketing machine.

www.cardratings.com is an invaluable web site…our source for credit card information. (US Citizens for Fair Credit Card Terms, Inc.) They are a grassroots consumer advocacy organization devoted to educating consumers about credit cards. They provide an independent source of consumer information and are not owned or governed by any banking or credit card interest. One of the primary methods they employ is providing consumers with ratings of credit cards. And much more…

CHAPTER 4

BANKING AND INVESTMENTS

No matter how we intend to run our personal finances, through checking, savings, or investments, we can save money.

CHECKING ACCOUNTS

1. Order the cheapest checks or the free ones. They do the same job as the more costly checks.
2. By not dropping below the minimum deposit required for an account, we save on service charges.
3. Purchase only those account benefits that we plan to use.
4. Get as much information about the account before opening it, to avoid confusion later. Ask about ATM and other fees, if they offer free checking, minimum balances required, personal computer banking options, and whether money earns interest and at what rate. Ask what other services are available such as credit card protection or life insurance, and the cost and fees.
5. Beware of payday mania when our checking account balances are highest. We may feel richer, and think we have money to spare. Try to reverse payday spending. Think as though it is the last

of the payday period instead of the beginning. Agonize in fun mode over each dollar spent. Tighten our belts. What a splendid surprise! At the end of the pay period we see a much larger balance. We have extra money to save.

SAVINGS ACCOUNTS

Interest rates fluctuate from one institution to another and within each institution. Various savings plans offer different rates. Investigate all kinds of savings accounts. Pick the best one for you. Don't be caught short down the line, by finding out our savings account is earning the least amount of interest in our area.

Some savings accounts come with a checkbook or a debit card. If savings is a new part of our life and difficult at best, opt for a savings account without a checkbook or debit card. Having a checkbook or debit card gives us the capability to sabotage our saving goals.

Author's scenario: During the late 1970s, between my divorce and remarriage, I had $1,000 in savings. I felt rich. I decided to take my children on a vacation to Unicoi State Park, in the mountains of northern Georgia. The cost, including airfare and car rental was about $550. However, upon our return home, I became ill and needed surgery. I was out of work for six weeks and before I knew it, the rest of my savings was spent. If my parents had not helped me financially, I don't know what I would have done. If I had known then what I know now, I never would have taken the vacation and depleted my savings account. I would have known that financial stability for my children was far more important.

DEBIT CARDS

Debit cards are used to pay for purchases. The amount is automatically deducted from a checking account at point of sale. They are more convenient and faster than writing a check. Word of caution: Upon purchasing, immediately deduct the amount from the checking account.

CREDIT UNIONS

Call several banks and credit unions to compare both savings and IRA interest rates. In September, 2006, in northwest Montana, savings accounts interest rates at banks fluctuated from .2% to .50%. Bank IRA interest rates fluctuated from 2.25% to 4.59%.

Credit union savings accounts interest rates fluctuated from 1.75% to 4.52%. Credit union IRA accounts ranged from 5.50% to 5.64%. Our credit union pays 1.50% over the savings rate. Neither banks nor credit unions charged a yearly fee for IRA accounts.

Outgoing wire transfers in banks ranged from $15.00 to $20.00, whereas credit unions charged the same price of $15.00. Be inquisitive. Get the facts. Put our money where it earns the highest rates.

INVESTMENTS

Investments are personal considerations. Before going into any investment, investigate the company as thoroughly as possible. Ask friends or family to refer us to reputable brokers. Get advice and opinions. Call the company and ask questions to familiarize us with the types of accounts and services they offer. Then research the company on the Internet.

Do invest in the best possible way. Some examples are: savings accounts, stocks and bonds, money market accounts, treasury notes, credit unions, or property. There are other options, as well.

If the stock market is chosen, there are various ways to do so. Choose a regular stockbroker, a discount broker, or try the Internet to decide the best one for our needs. Choose stock that has a positive growth history.

Risk is also a factor in choosing investments. Sometimes it is wiser to choose a secure lower rate investment, rather than, for instance, one that isn't insured by the government.

If we are planning to make a major purchase with part of our savings, wait until the interest received will pay for the item. Rule of thumb: Never withdraw from the principle. If possible, reinvest interest earned back into the principal.

Throughout our working years, periodically, calculate how much we will need in our retirement funds to live comfortably. Adjust contributions, as necessary. Do not borrow from IRA or 401(k) accounts.

CHAPTER 5

COMPUTERS

The best way we can save money on a computer is not to buy one unless we intend to make or save money by using it. If we know many friends, contacts, associates, relatives, etc, who also have computers, communicating through the Internet costs less than postage and phone bills. The Internet does not rely on the weather or time for delivery. It's a bit less personal than hearing voices, but allows for frequent interaction at less cost. Also, the Internet offers income opportunities and business options for entrepreneurs.

Many credit card companies, magazine subscriptions, banks, monthly billing services, mail order catalogs, and even online providers offer lower rates to customers who buy or pay online. Many companies that have online stores offer reduced rates and even offer free or no additional cost shipping and handling for online purchases. Most Internet shopping is cheaper for the consumer because of the reduced cost to the supplier, who does not need a store and associated overhead costs that the typical retail outlet has.

E-mail is free, not 42 cents or whatever the going postage rate is. Online chat on the Internet is often free.

We can shop via the Internet. However, a caution: Internet shopping can lead to overspending because it is so easy. PAA suggests a running list of purchase amounts be written down on paper that wraps around the credit card to be used for purchasing. This helps us to stay within our budget.

The Internet is the ultimate reference source for information. When was the last time you tried to cross reference research material using the Dewey Decimal system at our library? With a computer, all we need to do is type a keyword into a search site and get it all instantly, not just the material the library has on hand. Caution: Internet information isn't always accurate. Research is necessary to make sure we have a reliable site.

Value Added Service:

What is our time worth? Is it more valuable than dollars saved by spending extra dollars to find, receive, or wait for the product or service? Is three hours of calling and looking, and then waiting two weeks, worth more in dollar savings than finding an item quickly, getting it rapidly and not wasting all that time on it?

We value our time at let's say $5 an hour of work and $5 per day of waiting. Three hours of phone calls and inquires and waiting for someone to get back to us, and then 10 days waiting for the product with waiting time conservatively put at one hour per day: (3X5) plus (10X5) = $65. Or we can shop on the Internet and have it shipped the next day for $25. What is the value of expedience over time spent?

It all comes down to the level or speed of gratification we expect for our time and money. It may be a better value for us to wait and spend only time to get it, or it may be more satisfying to spend a few more dollars.

E-books can deliver new releases directly to us via download. If we like to read a lot, this can save us time at the bookstore, in addition to it being cheaper to download than to buy.

However, we can't lend an e-book to our neighbor. We can't fill a bookshelf with e-books. And you need to spend additional money up front to buy a peripheral to read the book anywhere you go.

My friend, Tanka, explained why she purchased each computer component and the reason she had for buying them. She didn't pay the asking price. She went to Radio Shack, told the salesman what she wanted and how much she had to spend. She needed more than her money would cover. The salesman and his boss worked with her and came up with a figure that she could afford. She saved over $1,200.

Another decision to make is to have high speed, DSL, or dial-up. If we use the computer for business, the high speed may be better. If we just use the computer for recreation, DSL or dial-up might be preferable because they're cheaper.

Should we have one phone line for the computer and our house or should we pay the extra money for separate lines? Does the time used on the computer warrant the extra expense? If it is not used for work, would it pay for itself? Do others in the household need phone availability all the time or can they use it around the computer use?

Recently, our telephone company offered DSL for $5 a month more than dial-up. It was well worth it. It came with an attachment to all phone jacks that enabled us to receive and make calls while we were online, even though we have only one phone line.

Whenever we need to purchase items for our computers, check Internet prices first. Then negotiate and compare prices with computer stores in our area. Never assume anything. We may think Internet purchases will cost less but until we compare prices, we will not know for sure.

CHAPTER 6

ENTERTAINING AND RECREATION

Entertaining? No matter what kind of entertaining or recreation we decide on, there are ways to cut back, save money, and still enjoy ourselves. Remember that our guests are there to enjoy our company and have a good time, not to be impressed with how expensive the spreads are.

Here are some suggestions:

1. Use regular dishes, cutlery and table covering. If we must use paper or plastic, buy plain, not decorated. It's cheaper. Spruce it up with homemade decorations.
2. Instead of liquor or champagne ("Ouch, this hurts. Everybody serves these drinks."), serve tea, coffee, soda, water, sparkling cider, or punch. Serve them with a different flare. Offer unusual herbal teas, flavored water, multi-flavored coffees, cappuccinos, ginger ale with fruit, and uncommon fruit additions to punch. Apple cider is yummy served with a cinnamon stick.
3. Serve simple desserts with different side selections, like cheeses on apple pie, or a variety of nuts, fruits and chocolate sprinkles to top ice cream. Banana slices and berries taste delicious mixed with yogurt.

4. Instead of pizza, have relish, vegetable, and fruit trays. Offer a large salad with chicken strips instead of meat as the main course. Serve them salad bar style. Guests gobble this up.
5. Purchase foods and drinks in peak season when prices are cheaper and they taste the best.

Before spending money on planned entertainment or recreation, think of a less expensive way of accomplishing the same level of enjoyment.

If our heart's set on going to that special place, plan ahead for the expenditure. Pay cash. Using a credit card should not be an option.

Restaurants:

Eating out can put our finances in jeopardy. We need to assess the reasons we dine out.

1. Do we do it out of habit?
2. Do we do it because it's easier than cooking at home?
3. Do we do it out of the need for sustenance when we are not near home?
4. Do we do it just for fun?
5. Or do we do it as a luxury treat?

What is our restaurant tab each month? Is it enough to reach our monthly saving goal or to make a huge dent in paying down credit card debt? Are we going out for dinner for no other reason than to get out? Is it an extravagance? Is our budget already squeezed? Are we using our credit card? Are we trying to impress someone? Before PAA we would go, pump up the credit card balance, and then panic when the bill came.

Still have a strong urge to eat out? Visualize the scales of justice. One side of the scale, if we eat out, it will tip toward higher credit card debt. But the other side, when we think about reaching an important goal, and we save the cost of dinner, the scale is more heavily tipped. Having made our decision, we feel exuberant, not deprived.

After learning PAA, we now decide to have an impromptu potluck dinner at home. Any concoction of foods will do. Make a fun combination of foods we have never had before, even if company is coming. Let them help with humor and imagination. While enjoying the meal, our mind wanders, happily concluding that we have not only saved money but we had fun to boot.

John and I go out for dinner twice a year. We don't feel deprived. The two times we do eat out, we relax and enjoy ourselves. We pay cash, and we don't worry about credit card charges. For those of us that eat more frequently at restaurants, add the total amount spent for a year. Would we prefer to have that money to use for essentials, where it counts, so as to reach our financial goals?

Ordering appetizers and desserts can quickly add to the total bill. Usually restaurants give bigger portions of the main course than we can eat. So why order extra items that contribute to both a bigger bill and feeling too full and bloated? Asking for a doggy bag is prudent. There's no stigma attached. We paid for it. It's ours.

Alcoholic beverages are another big expense. Before going out, have sparkling cider; with the meal, order water, tea or soda. Yes, we can eat out without ordering alcoholic beverages! If we must drink, do it at home after dinner. Restaurants benefit from the high cost of our drinking tab. We don't.

If the budget doesn't allow for a celebration dinner out, stay home, make a nice cozy dinner, reminisce, communicate, tell stories or play our favorite game. Enter PAA.

Other ways of saving on restaurant tabs: Go to a less expensive restaurant. Order a less expensive entrée. Choose a restaurant that has complete dinner prices, not an ala-carte one, where we pay for each item ordered. Multiple savings here: once on the total bill and again on a smaller tip.

Before eating out as a family unit, inquire if there are children's menus and if they are discounted or free.

If the restaurant has valet parking, use it only for emergencies or safety. Park our own vehicle and walk.

When we have company: If guests offer to treat us to dinner out, offer them a good home cooked dinner instead. If they insist, then happily go. It is not our duty or responsibility to treat guests to restaurant meals. Of course, if it doesn't put stress on our budget, then it is always a nice thing to do.

Fast Food Restaurants: These restaurants, however quick and inexpensive they may be, offer little as far as a healthy fare. Figure how much money we spend at these restaurants in a year. Then realize how much better it would have been if we had purchased fresh fruits or vegetables with whole grain crackers or bread.

A PAA lesson: Why would we consider grabbing a bite out to eat when we have unpaid bills? In the movies we see this practiced. It's a script. The writer's have the story worked out. It's not real life.

OTHER ENTERTAINMENTS

Going to a park that has an entrance fee? Park outside and walk in. It's usually cheaper. If we frequent a particular park, ask for a seasonal pass that allows us unlimited park use.

Picnics: Trim expenses. Take home cooked foods as opposed to store bought. Fried chicken is less expensive to make at home. Even cheaper, make a salad and toss in leftover chicken pieces. Throw together homemade cold slaw and potato salad, and include fresh fruit and freshly baked cookies. Peanut butter and jelly sandwiches on whole wheat bread are healthy and inexpensive, as well.

Video or movie rentals:

Hypothetically, we spend "just" $4.00 a week on video rentals. What's $4.00 anyway? Added up over a year, it comes to $208. A wiser choice would be to purchase tapes on sale for under a dollar apiece. On a 6-hour tape, we could tape three movies of our choice. That's about 33 cents per movie. By building up a library, we will be able to view them at our leisure, and save dollars. We may counter and say, "But there's a new movie we must see."

Whoops, here comes PAA. Do we really need this? Can we survive without it? If we wait a while, it'll come on TV. We can tape it ourselves. This isn't a hard decision after all. We save money. It's a good feeling.

If we want to go to the movies, attend a matinee. It's cheaper. If we can't go to a matinee, don't go at all. Do something else for free. Wait for the movie to be on TV. Remember, we are saving money. Give us a high five!

Before attending matinees, prepare some beverage, snacks and popcorn at home to take with you. The selections of these items at the theater can be expensive. See how many different ideas you can come up with. Change the menu with each movie you see. However, some theaters may not allow this practice. Try carrying small treats in our pockets.

Explore non-spending activities that alleviate impulsive comfort expenditures:

1. Visit a friend
2. Work on projects
3. Play games, work on a puzzle, or take up a hobby
4. Relax
5. Look at photo albums and reminisce
6. Exercise, jog or go for a walk
7. Watch a video
8. Go to a park
9. Write letters

10. Visit the library, read and learn
11. Go to a museum or an art gallery
12. Window shop
13. Attend discussion groups
14. Attend a free concert
15. Spend quality time with our children
16. Enjoy our computer
17. Join a club
18. Go to the beach
19. Get to know our neighbors
20. Enjoy what we have. Dwell on what we have, not on what we don't have.
21. In the fall of the year John and I sit in our vehicle on the side of a country road that has gold and red leaf arches. The gentle breeze coaxes the leaves to separate from the trees and they dance downward on wind currents until they come to rest on the leaf- covered ground. We listen carefully as some hit the roof of the truck. This is natures beautiful offering and it is free.

See how many more things you can add to the list.

CHAPTER 7

NOURISHMENT

As chapter 1 stated, when I was growing up in the '40s and '50s, my mother taught me where to save money. She said, "Everywhere but on food." However, when she took my brother, sister, and me grocery shopping, she showed us how to compare prices to get the best deal but she always shopped from a list of foods for weekly recipes. For instance, if she wanted to make salmon, she'd buy it, regardless, if a cheaper alternative fish were available. She always fed us well-rounded, nourishing meals that included protein, greens, and carbohydrates. It wasn't until I became an adult that I realized I could eat just as healthy while saving money on food.

The following are ways positive attitude adjustment teaches us to save on food:

1. A food is advertised two for $4.00. We automatically think we must buy two in order to get the sale price. Usually, we don't. We can buy one for $2.00. Occasionally, one item of a double item purchase might cost a few cents more that half.
2. Foods that come in small-necked bottles insure the manufacturer that, because it's too time consuming to scrape the contents out, the consumer will throw the unused portions away with the container, thereby causing the user to purchase the product more often. Some

of these products are catsup, mustard, and barbeque sauce. Instead of tossing them out with food still inside, place the container upside down until all the food moves to the opening. Then use the product with ease. Even when we think these containers are empty, add a little water, shake and add it to hamburger meat and meatloaf. Throw a little marketing strategy in our corner.

3. Not only can we stretch the use of foods, we can also start saving the crumbs from cereals, crouton packages and nut containers. Use bread, croutons and cereal crumbs for hamburger meat dishes and for thickening soups. They add delicious flavor. Use nut crumbs in baking recipes, such as banana breads, and cookies, storing them in freezer containers until they are needed.
4. Buy canned foods on sale by the case. Even if there's no case sale, sometimes the store will give a case discount. The store doesn't have to pay the employee labor costs of unpacking the merchandise and stocking it on the shelves.
5. Check prices on cold cereal and how many servings per box. Then check hot cereals, such as oatmeal (which contains outstanding nutritional values) and price per serving. Oatmeal is by far the better buy. If our preferences are still for cold cereal, buy it in large bags instead of boxes. It's cheaper. How much does a bowl of oatmeal cost in a

restaurant? $2.50 - $3.00. Add a tip and the total equals enough store bought oatmeal for four to five months!

6. Some supermarkets offer a point system that may save us money. This is fine. But be aware of our list and budget. Spending money on items we don't use or that aren't on our list increases the total bill and wreaks havoc on our budget.
7. Buy giant economy sizes. If these are too big, heavy or awkward to handle, put some in smaller containers at home. I do this with dishwashing detergent, cooking oils and soy sauce. Smaller sizes cost more. Be aware of expiration dates. If we are sure we can use up the product before the expiration date, then buy it. If not, purchase the smaller container.
8. Canning and freezing aren't for everyone, but it can be fun and rewarding knowing we are saving money. Buy fruits and vegetables on sale in peak season. The flavors are best and the prices are lowest. Some garage sales have inexpensive jars or give them away free. Use our ingenuity for other savings in this area or talk to others who do canning and freezing.
9. Eating foods just because they are advertised, or are part of a lifetime habit, doesn't make them nutritionally good choices. Unhealthy foods have been so widely accepted, we automatically think they are okay.

Foods in these categories can include processed foods, fried potatoes instead of baked, high-saturated fast foods, and high sugar content foods. The healthier we eat, the more money we save in future medical bills.

10. Keep track of the foods that are running low and try to catch a sale. If we do run out of a food and dash to the closest store, we will probably spend retail or higher.
11. We generally shop at two main supermarkets. But when others have sales of items that are on our list, we go there and do not feel guilty.
12. Utilize sales in different ways by buying in quantity. Make soup, baked goods, casseroles, and lasagna, and freeze them for later use. I bake a whole turkey, eating it for several meals, and then slice and freeze the leftovers to use as sandwich meat. A whole turkey costs less than $1 a pound, whereby sandwich turkey at a deli sells for $5.99 and more per pound. Idaho instant mashed potatoes cost $1.19 for 4oz and the list of chemicals is as long as my arm. A 10-pound bag of fresh potatoes cost $1.29.
13. Instead of making our weekly menus in advance, and shopping for the ingredients, do it in reverse. Check the food ads in the newspaper and make menus around what's on sale.
14. Sunday newspapers usually come with food coupons. Clip out the ones

normally used or ones we have been meaning to try. Compare them with supermarket ads and make our own list. By combining "cost us less" ways, we will save even more. Food coupons are a mainstay for saving money. Try http://www.coupon.net for food and other merchandise savings ideas.

15. We have all baked a whole chicken and thrown away the skin and bones. Now we put them in a pot of water, adding celery, onion and a carrot and simmer for an hour. Discard everything except the stock and refrigerate overnight. Skim off the fat from the top of the broth and store in freezer containers for use in soups, stews, rice and any other ways we can think of. We get more vitamins and minerals and the dish tastes better, as well. Likewise, when cooking vegetables, save and freeze the stock. It's good as a stir-fry base instead of oil, and makes soups that taste great. Canned minestrone soup can cost a lot. I copied down the ingredients reducing the salt, bought them, made a dozen quarts (utilizing frozen stocks), saved oodles of money, and it was healthier.
16. When preparing foods for freezing, the colder they are before being placed in the freezer, the less electricity it takes in the freezing process.
17. Thinking of purchasing a vacuum sealer machine to put frozen foods into? Try using freezer zip lock bags instead; zip them almost closed, stick a straw in the

small opening while sucking the air out, and then close the bag completely. We have just saved the cost of the machine and it's easier to do. If we only want a portion of the contents and wish to refreeze the rest, we don't have to drag the machine out.

18. Use teabags twice.
19. Get used to drinking water. Soda, liquor, beer, coffee, and tea cost money. Hypothetically, if we buy one soda a day from a machine at 75 cents a can for five days, the total is $3.75. That's $195 a year! A sensible alternative is to carry a thermos of water from home. Use PAA. We are the ones benefiting!
20. Cook fresh foods, not prepackaged. It's cheaper and more nutritional. Fresh fruits are also less expensive than canned, especially if you purchase them on sale during the height of the season.
21. Snack foods are not an option. Buy fruits and raw vegetables instead. For the cost of one bag of potato chips, which lasts less than a day, buy baby peeled carrots, bananas, or four apples for the same price. They'll last all week, and they're better for you, too!
22. Buying frozen hash brown potatoes at $1.29 on sale that serves four people? We spend $12.90 when buying the amount of servings that a ten-pound bag of potatoes gives us for 59 cents.
23. Reuse grocery shopping bags. A store near us credits us five cents a bag.

24. Use leftovers as soon as possible (before they turn into a hodgepodge of unidentifiable slimy green bacteria).
25. Buying a half-gallon of ice cream at $4.29 is more reasonable than ordering two scoops at a specialty parlor for $3.25.
26. Utilize banana sales the same way as with chicken. We buy riper ones, with their sweet rich flavor, for 29 cents a pound. Make breads, cakes and cookies to freeze. Certain times of the year there are big baking ingredient sales. Bake up a storm with the sale items and have inexpensive desserts all year.
27. Make lemonade from bulk jars of concentrate as opposed to frozen or fresh lemons.
28. Buy bulk cheese and grate it or instead of buying cut up meats for stir-fry, purchase larger pieces and cut them our-selves. Too tired to cook after a long day at work? Want to pop a store-bought frozen dinner in the microwave or eat take-out or snacks? Practice PAA. Try this instead: Take a frozen meal (that we made ourselves from foods we bought on sale) out of the freezer. While it's heating, unwind by singing a song or dancing. Keep homemade frozen hamburgers and sliced meatloaf in the freezer. These are easy to reheat. When we have time to cook our favorite dish, make double portions and freeze one.

29. Compare prices from store to store. I found canned black beans for $1.18 in one store and 66 cents for the same brand in another store.
30. If the outlying areas of our community have U pick farms, go. Have fun and save gobs of money.
31. If we don't look at food ads, and only shop at one store, we are overspending. By scouring ads and shopping sales at several stores, we can cut a great deal of money from our total food bill.
32. Stretch meals, even for company! Most of us have a main dish of meat and all the trimmings, but the meat is the most prominent, and the most costly. Try purchasing less meat and use it as a garnish, with the less expensive vegetables and carbohydrates such as rice, potatoes or pasta as the main dish. Then toss toothpick shapes of meat on top. Other examples are stir-fries, stews, baked assorted vegetables, spaghetti and meat sauce instead of meatballs.
33. Flavored water? Carbonated water? We have lived our entire life without them. Why start now? Just because it's the latest trend or because they taste good? Water out of a spigot (unless ours is contaminated) is free.
34. As we use up store bought condiments, herbs, and spices, save the containers to fill with items from bulk and discount stores. After researching for years, usually the best prices come from bulk stores or discount stores.

Supermarkets have the highest prices, even with 50% off sales!

35. Examples

ITEM	BULK STORE	SUPERMARKET	DISCOUNT STORE
Cardamom	$1.40 oz	$7.50 oz	N/A
Ground cloves	$0.95 oz	$1.12 oz	whole .717 oz
Onion powder	$0.35 oz	$2.50 oz	N/A
Sage	$0.75 oz	$8.74 oz	N/A
Thyme	$0.50 oz	$4.39 oz	N/A
Basil	$0.40 oz	$9.98 oz	.468 oz

Bulk isn't necessarily cheaper 100% of the time. It pays to compare prices. Buy just enough bulk herbs to last a short time. Fresher is better.

36. In recipes we add the exact amounts of ingredients. However, I've learned to use less nuts, chocolate chips, and raisins. The baked goods still taste good and I have saved money. If we learn we have a choice to use less than the suggested amount, we'll need only to purchase that product once a year instead of three times a year.
37. Generic and supermarket store brand items are less expensive than national brand names. Our store had a comparison testing of their brand and a national brand and asked which we preferred. Surprisingly, we liked all the store brand items better than the higher priced national brands.
38. While waiting in line to check out, ask ourselves if we need everything in our

carts or if we have included impulse items. Keep our needs. Leave unwanted items with checkout cashier. Watch as our food goes through the scanner. Some sale items may ring at the regular retail price.

39. Sometimes my husband John is so penny-pinching with money, he drives me crazy. For instance, I'd pick up halibut on sale in the supermarket. We had the money for it but he'd say we have tuna and canned salmon in the house and they are cheaper. I had to agree. It's these very decisions that allow us to save money every month.
40. We wanted a pasta dinner but didn't have sauce. We use pasta sauce from the health food section of our store. It doesn't have chemicals, sugar or bad fats, but it wasn't on sale. We put our dinner on hold until the sauce went on sale a few weeks later.
41. When we are young and vigorous, that's the time to eat healthy. We should not wait until a disastrous disease strikes, forcing us to give up unhealthy eating habits.
42. Are we running out of food before payday? Live on baked potatoes for a few days. John did this, not because he had to, but it meant more to him to protect his savings than to have a big meal.
43. As shopping lists are made, make out a separate one for items that can be purchased less expensively at discount

stores. It's so easy to incorporate these items in a grocery list if we are not aware we have choices. Many dollars are spent uselessly for higher prices at grocery stores.

44. Author's scenario: In the supermarket, I observed a young mother with a small child pondering whether to buy a prepackaged pasta dinner. Then she put it in her cart without another thought. I couldn't help wondering if she realized it was not a healthy product. After she walked on, I took the same pasta dinner box from the shelf and looked at the ingredients. There was white flour, hydrolyzed protein, 750mg of sodium, and many chemicals. I'd like to think, had the young mother had more healthful knowledge, she would have chosen a comparablely priced healthier alternative for her family.

Another scenario: I was in line at a drug store. A young mother with her daughter was ahead of me. The mother bought cigarettes, colorful chemically dyed candy, and flavored waters. She gave her toddler daughter a bottle of blue colored water to drink. I gagged at the thought that any parent would give such an unhealthy drink to their child when so many healthy alternatives are available (plain water, fruit juice, or milk). These alternatives not only make a healthier child but they are cheaper than what the mother bought. And I could not help but think of her daughter inhaling secondhand cigarette smoke. How much does the mother spend on cigarettes? Is it enough to pay for her daughter's college? Is it enough pay for the agony of seeing her daughter come down with asthma, lung or breast cancer, due to her smoking? Are the sugar-filled snacks and beverages enough for her daughter to acquire childhood diabetes? The financial consequences from both the smoking and the unhealthy diet are monumental.

45. Another money saver: buy bakery goods and breads at bakery outlet stores.
46. Buy one. Get one free. Most of these sales charge retail price for the first one. Be aware. Know our prices. Another store may have a sale on the same product and buying two would be cheaper than buying one and getting one free. For instance: buy one at 89 cents and get one free. The cost for the same product at the second store is three for $1.00.
47. Perhaps if we all boycotted foods with unhealthy ingredients, the manufacturers would ultimately take notice and offer us healthier choices. There would be less disease, fewer medical bills, and more money saved.
48. Cantaloupe: A container of pre-cut cantaloupe costs $4.29 for 1¼ pounds. A whole cantaloupe weighing 3¼ pounds at 39 cents a pound costs $2.27.
49. A 12-pack of soda costs $4.99. If we drink one pack a week during a 40-year career, it costs over $10,000.

If the ideas presented so far seem daunting, or even impossible, do not be overwhelmed. It took a long time for us to arrive in a state of debt; it will also take time to learn new attitudes and behaviors.

Positive attitude adjustment can be accomplished in steps. Make a few changes, and become comfortable with them. Later on, we can make a few more.

As we incorporate these changes into our routine, they will become habit and we will unlearn old destructive spending patterns. But we do not have to do this all at once. Just start somewhere and the effect of PAA will snowball.

Using this chapter's suggestions, widen our own personal food saving ideas and devise plans that work for us individually. There are no boundaries.

CHAPTER 8

LIFE CYCLE

This chapter will take us from infancy through old age. At each stage of the cycle there will be PAA financial suggestions geared for that particular group.

INFANCY THROUGH THE EARLY YEARS

Learning how to handle finances should begin at an early age. Parents can casually discuss ways to save money in front of their children. Play easy coin games with small change when children are young. Bring emotions and values into the game. Don't make a big deal of it. Also, discuss money matters in passing, in everyday tones. If there's yelling and screaming, the ideas we wish to instill will be rejected. Children will get used to hearing bits and pieces of finance and the knowledge will be stored away for future use. As they grow older the complexities and teachings of money management should be increased. I suggest setting aside time every week, in a family unit, to read aloud, chapters of this book, so all members benefit from the financial information. Include our children as we implement this book's ideas into our daily routine. When we wait until the teenage years to teach them, they will certainly rebel. They already have seen their peers acting unaware that there is a prudent way of handling money.

For my grandchildren's birthday and holiday presents, my daughter-in-law takes them to a toy store and walks around with them so they can choose what they want. After the first selection, if they see something else they want, she gives them a choice; do they want the first toy or do they want the second toy more? This teaches them how to think for themselves, how to make choices, and how to develop preferences. If they choose the less expensive toy, they get to save the difference to spend another day.

Teach children that some parents earn more money than others. However, this doesn't necessarily mean higher earning power is more important than lesser paying jobs. Children should be made aware that people in certain professional careers, such as lawyers, doctors, advertising executives, and CEOs of large companies have the potential to earn more money than those who work at white collar jobs, and manual labor jobs. A good education and hard work enable us to rise above meager beginnings and poverty.

Every family has problems. Having more money doesn't guarantee fewer problems. Sometimes children with the most money are unhappier inside than the kids with less. Teach children that having less to spend is nothing to feel inadequate about. Teach them not to poke fun at others less fortunate. Tell them how lucky they are to live in the USA compared to third world countries where people barely survive. Teach them that by studying, even when other children make fun of them for doing so, they will have opportunities to go to college. Knowledge brings financial security beyond any wild imagination.

Marketing strategies geared toward children can undermine parental authority. Being aware of this, we can avoid being caught in their net. Children's TV shows advertise new toys, games, and more, drawing them into the excitement of owning these new treasures. They don't, as yet, know how to distinguish between needs and wants, or understand the differences between reality and fantasy. Children are vulnerable. They will demand to have the new toys and games because their friends have them. They want to fit in, to be accepted.

Scenario: This is how Kelly handles children's TV shows and their commercials: First she trys to keep the kids busy as she records shows she wants them to see when they want to watch TV. The children do not have TV sets in their bedrooms, so Kelly knows when and what they are viewing at all times. Her oldest son, age 6, was a sucker for commercials. After a few attempts at getting Kelly to buy a cool advertised toy, she now says: "See, you cannot believe everything on TV. They are trying to get you to buy it so they can make money". His reply to the TV commercials: "You aren't tricking me to get my money."

When we have prior conversations about the value of money with children, as a matter of passing, they respond differently to advertisements. Children can dare to be different. They do not need to follow the beat of others, including how they spend money or buy toys. They will feel secure in setting their own agenda, knowing it is right for them. Guide them to emerge into what they are meant to be. Explain need versus want using food versus toys. Explain advertising pros and cons; that what others want us to have should not dictate what we purchase.

Peer pressure can be overwhelming for children. Before they are old enough to be exposed to this, parents should make children aware of this potential problem. When children are taught self-confidence, they are able to ward off detrimental suggestions and activities. They'll know how to say "No".

Take children shopping. Explain why we choose one brand over another and the money saved. Explain why we are shopping around for the best price. By experiencing these outings, children get a low-key education that will pave the way to their own financial success.

Teach children organizational techniques: hang like clothes together in closets, arrange similar toys together, keep dresser drawers neatly, have specific places to put things to avoid misplacing them, and keep money in a piggy bank or other container. Having these skills will help them keep their lives and finances orderly later on.

When purchasing large ticket items, explain our motives, as well; for instance, the better brand will last longer, it's safer, or the quality is better.

Examples of places to take children are grocery stores (introduce them to sales of the week through newspaper ads), big chain stores, retail stores, and discount stores (explain the differences in merchandise, price and quality). Go to dollar stores, newspaper and magazine stands, drug stores, real estate offices, music stores, mailing outlets, gas stations, travel bureaus, sporting good stores, pet shops, nurseries, hardware stores, and saddlery stores. The list is endless. Add more places that fit into our lifestyle. The more exposure children receive the more prepared they'll be as prudent adult shoppers. Pick a day with our kids for the sole purpose of going from one different store to another. Pack a picnic lunch. Have fun.

Introduce children to sewing and mending, including boys, and teach girls about carpentry and vehicle maintenance. They will need the knowledge later when they're on their own.

Introduce children to woodworking, painting, home repairs, maintenance, and music appreciation by the great masters in history. Show them the love of nature, smell the roses, walk in a garden, listen to the sounds of waves lapping the shoreline, and appreciate the beauty of new spring blossoms and autumn leaves. The healing powers of nature can help sustain and give peace within, during a crisis, and help us to relax from the stresses of the day. This remedy works better than drowning sorrows in alcohol, which costs money and can devastate health.

When my mother passed away, John and I stayed at an efficiency apartment on the ocean. The beauty of the water and its peacefulness helped soothe the worst heartache in my life.

Give our children as well-rounded lives as possible, including money smarts. If they find themselves in a financial quandary later in life, they'll be fortified with knowledge to help them through. When they leave home, giving them a copy of this book will also help.

Children's diet should be low in saturated fats, processed sugars and salt, while high in fiber, whole grains, vegetables and fruits. Snacks should be nutritious. Choose fruits, mini peeled carrots, rice cakes, or whole grain crackers. Eating well means being more alert and having greater energy levels to comprehend and do better in school, and to have stamina for exercising and staying healthier.

Teach children not to touch their eyes or mouth with their hands. This is the quickest ways to introduce germs into their bodies. Have children wash their hands with soap and water frequently throughout the day, whether at home, school, or out and about. The more they rid themselves of hand germs, the less frequently they'll get sick, which means fewer doctor and medication bills.

When buying beds for children, think about these suggestions:

1. Investment in a good mattress set is better than buying a larger bed.
2. Twin beds cost less than bigger ones. The savings continue through their childhood. Linens are cheaper, from the cost of sheets, to blankets and spreads. Drying time takes a shorter cycle, saving on electricity.
3. When buying children's furniture, buy styles for the future. If we buy styles for very young children, the child outgrows

it. Then another bedroom set needs to be bought.

Dental hygiene is important throughout one's life. Brush teeth thoroughly twice daily from childhood on. Have a children's dentist show them proper brushing and flossing techniques. Some kids may think that tooth decay happens to older people, but not to them. They need to be aware that this is not the case. They may get a little lazy and not do a good job. It's up to the parents to keep tabs on proper dental hygiene of the children.

I was lazy in dental hygiene during elementary school. My parents did not check my brushing. Multiple cavities cropped up. In the ensuing years, gum recession developed, a periodontal disease. From all the large fillings, the teeth began to crack and many crowns were needed. Subsequently, I required a root canal, and now because of gum recession, my teeth are deteriorating. My dentist strongly urged me to buy a Sonicare toothbrush that cost $100. I did, and that proved to be a good investment because both my teeth and gums are now healthier than they've been in years. To keep the periodontal disease in check, prescription toothpaste costs $15.00. I'm paying a high price for my dental hygiene laziness: well over $15,000 and still climbing.

Crowns are selling for over $850 now. Special periodontal care also is expensive. So please have our children adopt a healthy dental regime to prevent devastating future expenses.

ROLE MODELS

We need to find out whom our child chooses as a role model. Before they make the decision, we need to give children background knowledge that will guide them in making the right choice.

Role model choices for children:

1. Are they in the entertainment industry? Do they drink, drug, or smoke? Many live lavishly, flashing tangible assets, as if these expensive eccentricities are needed to feel accepted. Children are easily drawn into this kind of longing and envy, therefore, becoming dissatisfied with their own lifestyle. They may become depressed, withdrawn, frustrated, or angry. They have not yet learned what qualities are important. Choosing wrong role models can cost a lot. If, for instance, a rock star is chosen, that takes illicit drugs, children, wishing to emulate that star, would be enticed into taking illicit drugs, as well. It is sad, that in today's age, the disrespectful, condescending, and revered celebrities make headlines.
2. Before children have a chance to choose the wrong kind, be aware that role models need to be those that set good examples that we can teach our children. Tell them about great people who have extraordinarily contributed to mankind and the world. Great people have given of themselves to others, and have leaped impossible hurdles to accomplish what they have. Watching TV biographies or reading about worthy role models are two good ways. Eligible role models are limitless. The legendary golfer, Tiger Woods, puts family above all else. There is Mother Teresa, Thomas Edison, and thousands more.

3. But, the most important role models children need are their parents, and this includes being fiscally responsible. Worthy role models help lay the groundwork for positive responsive attitudes in many areas, such as making the right choices, learning fact from fiction, and knowing that skin-deep attributes of flaunting money, drugs and alcohol, are not qualities children want to emulate. Children need qualities that sustain them through life. To be taught character, integrity, honesty and self-worth gives children the impetus to strive toward a secure lifestyle, which includes the importance of money.

ALLOWANCES

Children's allowances are yet another tool to teach financial responsibility. There are no rules regarding the sum or how often it is given. However, do exhibit restraint on the amount and be prepared to give it on the day it is promised.

Judy's scenario: Do not give into children's whims when they want more money than has been decided upon. They may learn that $30 or $40 dollars a week is a great scam on parents, and that they'll always be able to scam parents out of more money by whining or pleading. Giving into them is not the way to teach the value of money. A much smaller amount, say $5.00 or $10.00 is more appropriate. If we choose, deposit the difference between the two amounts into a college fund.

Do expect children to "earn" their allowance by having them do household chores congruent with their abilities and ages. For instance, a five-year-old could not be expected to mow grass and trim bushes, whereas a teenager could easily do it.

How do we arrive on an allowance figure? Put our budget first, deciding how much we can afford, and take into consideration what purposes it will be spent. Set down firm rules and guidelines: curfews, chores, if money runs out before allowances are due, there will be no advances, and it is not to be spent on things that disparage family values. If the rules and guidelines are not respected, allowances cease. Tell children how we arrived at the allowance figure, what it will cover and what it will not cover. Some parents choose to buy all their children's clothes and school supplies while others include these expenditures within the allowance.

The more children know about intricacies of allowances, the more likely they will spend it wisely. Rich or poor, they need to respect the dollar amount and not throw it around frivolously. Money is not a joking matter! Teach them to spend a portion and save some toward bigger future purchases, for instance, a drum set, a birthday gift, or a school trip. These are good money management lessons. Allowance's main purpose is to give children a sense of self-worth and responsibility.

Parental incentives: Encourage our children to save part of their allowances by matching a portion of the amount they save.

When children want to supplement allowances, there are numerous options: wash neighbor's cars, cut lawns, walk dogs, help the elderly by doing yard work or housekeeping, assist a new computer user, or baby-sit. Strongly advise them to save all the money they earn, using allowances for everyday expenditures. Later, when they want to buy a car, they can help finance it with their saved money, a valuable lesson.

The best learning tool I have found to teach children about finances is "Free to Spend." It's a game that comes in

both a student and adult version. It shows how to budget money, and where to save and cut back in order to buy what is needed. The designer is Sharon Nash and she calls it "Mission Tool Kit." You can get in touch with her by using any of the following means:
TEL: 1-800-844-3710
Web: www.freetospend.com
Email: info@freetospend.com
P.O. Box 915, Kalispell, MT 59903-0915

Some children are not content with living simply if they aren't taught why it's best for them. It's not an easy task for parents, with TV shows, commercials and zillions of other fantasy stages showing wealth as the norm. Tell our kids, as a rule, TV shows do not depict real life scenarios. TV's main purpose is to entertain. Tell them if you lived lavishly, their college funds would not exist. Explain why and how they need to be satisfied with what they have and not to be envious of others who have more money. Tell them if they prefer a higher level of living, they need to study hard and go to college to learn a vocation that will give them a higher living income.

Let children know why we watch our finances. That if we didn't, there would be no vacations, emergency funds, savings, repair money, new vehicles, life insurance, or college funds. Explain a choice that might be taken is one parent staying at home to care for the children while the other works. If we lived a higher lifestyle, both parents would need to work and the school children would lose the anchor they now enjoy, by coming home to a parent instead of an empty house. We need to weigh our priorities and choose what's best for our family.

When children do extra chores far beyond the expected ones, make a chart, and give stars for each extra task. Give the monthly winner a prize. It could be anything from having their friends over for homemade cookies and listening to their favorite music, to a day out with family, one on one, a favorite supper, or doing something the child really wants to do. Do anything that's not expensive.

Later on, as working adults, they'll know if their job performance goes that extra mile, they'll earn a raise at evaluation time.

BIRTHDAY PARTIES

How sad, and when did these birthday celebrations get completely out of financial control? When did the simple family and friends' celebrations at home turn into major money spending escapades? (Going to fast food restaurants, hiring clowns, ventriloquists, entertainers, etc.) It's a bad signal showing children that whoever spends the most will be the most popular. We need to get back to teaching children proper values. Also, when a child cannot afford a birthday gift they can bring homemade cookies with a homemade card that includes a personal poem meant especially for the birthday child.

The birthday child should cherish this type of gift as much as the ones that cost more money. They should not make the poorer child feel uncomfortable. If anyone else does, the birthday celebrant should stick up for the poorer child, exclaiming the cookies are his or her favorite.

Imagine if our child invites 25 friends to a birthday party, that he will be invited to 25 parties. Even at $10.00 a gift, that's $250 a year. Imagine what disaster our budget would be like. PAA shudders. It sees the family savings dry up. Instead, PAA suggests reducing gift costs to $5.00 and putting the difference in a college fund.

SECONDHAND

When purchasing children's furniture and toys, be aware of the safety of each one, and examine them closely for flaws. Do research. Test the product. It may have a safety recall. When in doubt, don't buy. In the long run the money saved is not worth jeopardizing our child's safety. These same cautions apply to any secondhand purchase.

Children grow quickly. At times they outgrow three or four sizes a year! It could wreak havoc with our finances. To help alleviate this money crunch parents can start a new branch of PTA, a secondhand clothing outlet in a garage or other available facility. This would be for all children, regardless of economic status. When children need another size, drop off the child's outgrown clothes, choose larger garments, either free or for a couple of dollars, to be donated back to the PTA or to pay for facility operating costs. Instead of kids ridiculing others wearing their outgrown clothes, they can have fun guessing whose clothes they have. While in the planning stages, suggest that parents read this book, as to introduce them to this concept and to prepare the way for their kids to have an optimistic and entertaining approach to it.

Imagine how much money we would save! And secondhand clothes should be in good condition because children usually outgrow clothes way before they are worn out.

Positive attitude adjustment loves this concept. Deposit the saved money into a college fund.

In Queen's, New York, in the 1960s I was friendly with Tom and Beatrice. Even though they made above average incomes, they chose to live simply. She frequented secondhand stores, looked for bargains, and had fun doing it. When their daughter was born, instead of moving from their one bedroom apartment to a larger one that cost more money, they partitioned part of the living room for the nursery. She bought her baby's clothes at Carter's outlet stores and any other places she could get discounts. She and Tom had set plans and financial goals from the beginning of their marriage. They pinched pennies over the next several years, saving enough for a down payment on a beautiful home. To them, it was no sacrifice spending less. It was a way to achieve their goals.

THE EVERYDAYS OF GROWING UP

Children learn by observing their parents. Show them it is okay to pack a lunch for an outing or to go shopping. Homemade is cheaper, by far, than the cost of lunch at a restaurant. If we are caught without lunch, buy a piece of fruit or a whole wheat bagel. Teach children about restaurants, fast food, family style, mid and high priced. Explain when it's appropriate to go to each one, money-wise and social-wise.

Teach children monetary principles of a home-cooked meal versus going out and spending money. When we stay home, we tighten family relations, we talk about feelings, play games, watch TV, make popcorn with apple cider, look at family albums, tell family stories, start a garden and teach them how to care for and harvest it. Have one on one communications, urging each child to present us with a problem. Show them options for solving it, including money problems. Tell personal stories that are happy, sad, or funny. All these things are free.

Parents need to give factual explanations on why and how they save money. Explain the emotional and practical side and point out the differences. For instance, we can replace an original planned activity, such as a visit to an amusement park, with a less expensive alternative of seeing a movie. Or we can plan a free activity of splashing around with hoses flailing in our backyards and having a barbeque. When it rains, my daughter-in-law and my grandkids go puddle jumping.

When outings or plans need to be changed due to budget cuts or other reasons, children need positive explanations so as not to feel upset or deprived. Sweep children up into the new plans by showing they will be just as much fun. In the future, when money matters improve, the cost of going to the amusement park can be justified.

Children will have a better understanding of our financial teachings if we actually show them where money comes from and goes, and when it is saved. Explain the correlation between money earned from working and how that relates to how much we have to spend. The amount earned decides our lifestyle. The money left after the bills are paid is saved. Show them long-term choices for spending and investing: for instance, saving for a down payment for the family home, if renting at present, saving for college, a first vehicle, a new bicycle, a makeup vanity, a class trip, or a dirt bike. Ask children what they'd like to save for.

If our child has his heart set on designer brand jeans and jacket, such as Levi's or Nike, tell him, since the price exceeds the family clothing budget, he needs to pay the difference between the designer brand and the less expensive Carter or OshKosh brands. Or, beforehand, he could have learned enough about finances, that he wouldn't even consider buying the designer brand. He knows that clothes, no matter their cost, are just body coverings.

Parents need to take responsibility for teaching their children the value of a dollar. Friends don't do it. Schools don't do it. Make sure our children have a strong base for making the right financial choices. Teach them to solve their own money problems.

Have a contest with all the family members to see who comes up with the most money saving ideas. Children can observe friends' spending patterns, recognizing and learning right and wrong habits for their own lives. Figure out a low cost prize. Keep the contest alive. Each month, award a prize. The longer the contest remains a normal, constant activity, the more ways the child learns to manage finances.

If children feel uncomfortable telling their friends what their family is doing, they need not say anything. It can be a private family matter. They would not care to be ridiculed by their peers. However, if a friend thinks it's a really cool idea, perhaps that friend could join the group fun.

As children grow older, discuss within their hearing, the subject of retirement funds, if only to familiarize them with that aspect of life. When they're out on their own, they'll be fortified with that knowledge.

A favorite place where children love to hang out is at a mall where they socialize with friends. However, malls are designed by marketing geniuses to entice spending. I suggest, before children discover this means of socializing, gear them toward productive activities, such as reading books, making good grades, hobbies, sports, after school extracurricular activities, volunteer work, or part-time jobs. These time-consuming activities not only broaden knowledge, they teach joint effort, problem solving, and build character. Malls do none of these things. When children are busy with productive interests, they are not in malls spending money.

Parents, already overwhelmed with responsibility, may be too busy to guide children to productive activities. "We can't do everything." Think for a moment. Every idea in this book helps us and our children handle finances better. Incorporate ideas into everyday discussions while driving in the car, during meals, while doing chores and family activities. Even busy parents feel the need to teach their children everything they can, enabling them to be financially responsible. Let's make the effort. The results will amaze us.

TEENS, CREDIT CARDS AND FINANCES

Preteens need to know what lies ahead for them in as many ways as possible. Parents should talk to them about changes concerning what will be expected from them: for instance, keeping company with responsible kids that make good grades, as opposed to kids that make poor grades and have no respect for elders in authority. Tell them they are responsible to tell parents whom they are with, for what reason, and to respect curfews. And tell them the house rules are to be honored. Then when they become teens, they will know the ground rules, making the transition an easier one.

I believe the most difficult years for teenagers are ages thirteen through fifteen. These years are marked by many changes: in essence, the transition from childhood to adulthood. Teen's bodies change internally, hormones run rampant, peer pressure is at an all time high, and as a result of feeling bewildered, they put on a know-it-all front.

What does this indicate financially? It means, before reaching this age of conflicting emotions, teens need an understanding of what lies ahead. Parents must talk to them about positive aspects and opportunities of growing up, such as, what their vocational aspirations are, that good grades are needed to reach these goals, and what it takes to be accepted into college. Children need to plan their lives accordingly so as not to let outside forces interfere with future plans. Explain hormonal changes, and warn them if they act irresponsibly it not only can lead to disease or pregnancy, it can permanently alter future plans. Either of these possibilities can cause both emotional and financial chaos.

Scenario: Daughter, aged fourteen, rebelled against her parents. She thought she knew it all and they didn't know a thing. Her dad taught her not to question her mom's authority, so even though she was always available, daughter was scared to talk to her about controversial topics and feelings. Her hormones were in high gear and left her in a state of ambiguity. When she would hang out with friends, it seemed they had lots of money for movies and snacks, but she had to squeeze money from a meager allowance, which left her feeling inadequate and an outsider looking in. In front of family, daughter pretended everything was fine, but in reality she wanted to scream out for help. Instead, she was quietly defiant, resentful, unhappy, and confused.

Prepare children both financially and emotionally for these difficult years by laying the groundwork ahead of time. Wouldn't a parent be proud if their child, who did not have a lot of spending money, had self-confidence to say "no" when friends wanted to spend money on inconsequential frivolities? And when our teenagers are pushed toward sexual activeness, they have fortitude to say "no" to that, as well.

If teens know uncertainty is part of transitioning to adulthood, and they have an open relationship with parents, they experience fewer emotional and financial difficulties.

Teens need to learn about checking and savings accounts as well as proper use of credit cards.

Show them what a check looks like. Explain how to write a check, keep a register, how to balance it each month, where the routing number is and what it is for, and the consequences for overdrawing. To prevent possible fraud from someone changing the check amount, explain by writing the written amount of the check as close as possible to the left on the line, there is less room to alter figures. The same rules apply to writing number amounts. Everything written on a check needs to be clear and legible. And remember to show them the proper way to endorse the back of a check. Their signature should be written as close to the top of the check as possible.

Teens should have a savings account, as well. It helps if a parent accompanies them to the bank to open their first account. They will learn what information and minimum balance is needed to open the account, how to chose a title, fill out a deposit slip, acquire interest rate knowledge, and how to compare other kinds of saving instruments, such as certificates of deposit and money market accounts that offer higher rates of interest than regular savings accounts.

Buying teens a birthday or holiday gift of stocks in their favorite interest is a great financial teaching tool. My son received utility stocks as a gift for his thirteenth birthday. He was able to learn not only about his stock, but other aspects of investments.

Teach them the fundamentals and pros and cons of credit cards. Cards are to be used responsibly. If they pay interest, it is throwing money down the drain. Money saved from not paying interest covers emergencies or goes toward reaching goals.

Emphasize the importance of paying balances in full each month. To do otherwise is not an option. Tell them good credit ratings open financial doors, such as acquiring a mortgage and car loans at lower rates. Bad credit ratings haunt us for years, causing great difficulties and embarrassment, and lead to bankruptcy, as well.

Credit card introductory rates may be low for a while, but invariably increase. Work with children until they understand about credit card usage. By using PAA, they will be steered in the right direction to achieve credit card fitness.

I suggest giving children their own credit card in the senior year of high school before they go off to college. It helps if they have a part-time job. Give them a low limit. Discuss the differences between wants and needs. Is a new outfit worth more than college tuition and books? Never charge up to the limit. Always have leeway to cover unexpected contingencies.

A teens' first vehicle: Before children reach driving age, parents need to talk about responsibilities that go along with ownership. Having a vehicle is a privilege to be earned (good grades maintained and chores done in a timely manner, and show respect for family values and rules).

My friend Eleanor's grandson, Tom, age 16, works part-time to pay the expenses for his first car. He bought an old clunker but to him it was a big deal. He followed all the rules his parents set, kept his grades up, did all his chores, and was a responsible driver. So when his father needed to replace the family car, he made a deal with his son. Tom could have the old family car if he paid him the trade in cost in monthly payments from his part-time job. Tom learned an important lesson in PAA from his father.

The Federal Deposit Insurance Corporation offers a free Consumer Newsletter, *Start Smart: Money Management for Teens - How to Save, Spend, and Protect Your Cash.* It includes money management for teens, everyday things teens can do to save money, how small savings can grow big over time, where to keep money (banks, credit unions, etc.), describes stocks, bonds, savings bonds, and mutual funds, ways to cut spending and still be cool, explains loan responsibility, ways to avoid identity theft, and explains the roles of the FDIC and banks. To order this or get more information, go to www.fdic.gov or call 1-877-275-3342.

Preparing teens for college should start at an early age. (This is another topic that parents should discuss within hearing distance of young ears). Talk about their vocational aspirations and how good grades help them attain those goals, even though they may not yet know what they want to do. Explain about finding a ratio between spending and saving, so they can plan ahead to reach their goals. While in high school show them how to plan in advance for funds to cover books, computers, spending money, and tuition. Have them think ahead as to which universities offer their field of study, and what criteria the university has for acceptance.

A survey of Flathead Valley, Montana, straight A high school seniors, asked what their secrets were for attaining the highest scholastic grades. The most frequent replies were: "parental encouragement, involvement, and support in both academic and personal life; keep focused and study hard, but don't get burned out; do all homework to the best of my ability; an inquisitiveness to learn everything I can; not being afraid to ask for help from teachers; and fortitude."

Parents, let's learn from the best. These straight A students are giving us a road map to success to help our own children achieve the highest grades. If we start ingraining these bits of wisdom while our children are young and we consistently follow through as they grow older, we will be giving them the greatest tools to succeed.

DATING

For anyone who dates, here are some guidelines:

If our dates say, "I love people in jeans," or doesn't like our hairstyle, or wants us to wear their favorite color, stop and think! This information tells us they are skin deep. They may not possess the inward qualities that are so much more important (personality, integrity, caring, honesty). Think what this information means to the future relationship and to our pocketbook. Hypothetically, we could go out and purchase all the *things* that makes our date happy, while our credit card balance increases. Don't be pulled into this nightmare. People, as a rule, do not wish to have relationships with shallow people. We need to be ourselves and find someone who likes us for us, not for what we wear or how we comb our hair. We will save money and heartache.

Some people may expect to be wined and dined. Maybe this is what they consider important. Again, stop and think. Wouldn't we rather have a relationship with a person who considers and respects our existing lifestyle? We save money on a down-to-earth relationship versus a high lifestyle pursuit.

Places to go and activities widely vary in the dating scene. Going on errands with a date can lead to understanding his or her traits, preferences, and other ideas. We could also learn our date's economic values.

Going for walks, exercising, having picnics, and cooking a homemade meal are excellent choices for getting to know someone. Going out to a nice restaurant, but not necessarily an expensive one, for special occasions also works well.

On the other hand, movies or loud discos offer limited quality conversation time.

Dating is an important money spending activity. It could play a vital role in future relationships. If we were a middle-income person, we wouldn't want to marry anyone bent on a high spending lifestyle. We need to be economically compatible. The key to a lasting relationship is getting to know the person, not how much is spent.

Scenario: Hyrone, who is mesmerized with Shada, wants to impress her on their first date. He lives on a tight budget and has little to spend on recreation. However, Shada has turned his head to the point that he is walking around in a trance. He allows his otherwise good caution to be blown away. To impress Shada, Hyrone goes to a fancy men's boutique with deliberate intent and buys a designer suit, shirt, tie, cologne, and shoes, on credit. And he takes her out to dinner at an expensive restaurant.

Hyrone learns a lesson soon enough, when his relationship with Shada dissolves and he has to pay for the new clothes and dinner that he charged. John never spent lavishly on dates and he wore what he had.

YOUNG ADULTS AND COLLEGE

If money is not available to attend a four-year university, we can choose to attend a community college, which is less expensive. But, before doing that, students need to make sure that the university of their choice, which they will transfer to at the end of two years, will accept credits from the community college.

College financial assistance is available through grants, good grades, sports, and other interests, scholarships, and financial aid.

Before attending any higher education facility students should know the value and purpose of a credit card and be mature enough not to abuse it. It would help, too, if they reread this book right before leaving home, so they have PAA in the forefront of their minds.

We hear from the media how many people are abusing credit cards. Some young adults will assume, by not being under parental supervision, they can go on a free-for-all charging spree.

Remember, when young adults leave the household, it's usually their first time away from home. Everything is a new experience. The more knowledge we give them beforehand, the better acclimated they will be as they settle into living on their own.

Do not let ourselves be the parents who pay all college expenses, only to have their child charge thousands of dollars on credit cards while at school. If parents pay their child's credit card bills, a limit should be imposed to fit the parent's budget. College students can work part-time to help defray costs. There is also no harm done if they have a checking account and no credit card.

Discuss with our young adult beforehand the appropriate action if they receive an unsolicited credit card in the mail while at college. Using it is not an option. Should they call parents immediately, cut up the card, or send it to the parent to handle? Make rules and stick to them.

There are many roads to life on the horizon for young adults. But no matter where they go or what they do, they will emerge with enough financial skill to sustain them through life, if we have given them fundamentals when they grew up.

As they go out into the work world, they are fortified with knowledge in their choice of living quarters, career wardrobes, buying a vehicle, and in budgeting. They will not be one of thousands who immediately drown in credit card debt by purchasing unneeded items or everything they need at once.

If young adults, having lived a PAA lifestyle, need a loan, and can't get one from a bank or other reputable source, they are able to think of other alternatives. Asking parents for loans should not be an option, especially if the young adult earns more than the parent.

As they begin careers, it is imperative to take full advantage of retirement plans offered by employers, contributing the maximum allowed. This increases nest eggs while lowering taxes. With so many companies cutting back on both retirement and medical benefits, we urgently need to help ourselves in every way we can.

PRE-MARRIAGE

Things discussed prior to marriage often set the stage for reality checks, which lead to a successful or a failed relationship. Both parties need to communicate about many different topics that affect their future lives. One of the biggest issues is that of finances. It's important at this time to come together with a plan that is mutually acceptable and beneficial to both parties. Consider financial goals, a shared workable budget, mutual ideas for cutting back, and how to handle situations that tempt us to overspend. There needs to be full honesty. Any cover-ups or apathetic attitudes could lead to later problems. Discuss both salaries, if both are working, how and who will handle the money, how it will be dispersed, and common goals.

How should extra pocket money be handled? Will there be optimistic support for our spouse's choices for wisely spending money, or pessimism? If there is a difference of opinion, communicate. Do not shout! Compromise. Explain feelings and thoughts. Sometimes suggestions show us how to do the same thing cheaper. Will our partner be receptive, angry, or sweep financial problems under the table? It's better to find out before marriage exactly what both of our financial goals are. Make sure they are compatible. One may enjoy city life, and value social status and expensive clothes, while the other enjoys home entertainment and is content with a simple lifestyle. Remember finances are the leading cause of divorce.

A significant topic to discuss: How much credit card and other debt does each party bring into the marriage? Would it scare us if the person we were planning to marry has $43,000 outstanding on a credit card? Would we be held responsible for their debt? Would this pattern of charging continue to escalate after marriage? Do we make enough money to pay off what our prospective partner owes and how many years would it take? Are we prepared to assume that kind of responsibility? If starting married life with someone that is deeply in debt scares us (which it should), reality says do not marry this person. Rationalizing this situation will be disastrous later on.

There are enough disagreements, even in a good marriage, without making money the main cause. So if debt does come with the onset of marriage, have a mutual plan and time frame to pay it off.

If the wedding is to be paid for by the bride and groom, it should be paid for with funds available, not with credit cards.

Scenario: Kevinee's fiancé, Grelinda, insisted on a $40,000 wedding and a $15,000 marquise shaped diamond engagement ring. She had dreamed of owning such a ring and having a fairy tale extravagant wedding since she was a little girl. She equated all this with how much Kevinee loved her. She had no conception of the reality of such warped fantasies. Since Kevinee loved her so much he wanted to please her in every way, but since he had made the positive attitude adjustment transition, there was no way he could go along with such irresponsible behavior. He realized that if Grelinda really adored him, she would not want to put them so deeply in debt. The true test of love is taking care of one another in every way, including living debt-free. They did not get married. (If Kevinee had $55,000 he would have been wiser to buy a house or invest it, not blow it on a fantasy.)

We would all like to have champagne money for our champagne tastes, but life is not a fairy tale. Being content with less benefits us.

Weddings, no matter how big or small, or how much is spent, do not guarantee a long happy life. Even in the pre-marriage stage, both parties need to have compatible future financial goals.

When planning a wedding, stay within the budget. Many couples opt for expensive weddings and pay for it for many years to come. This is impractical and lays the groundwork for resentment, which can ultimately ruin a marriage.

In addition, seriously, think about bridesmaid's dresses. There are the traditional styles that scream out "I am a bridesmaid dress." Show consideration for bridesmaid's finances and choose a style that can be worn many times. Investing in a dress, shoes, purse, shower and wedding gifts, and transportation and motels are costly enough.

Diamond engagement rings are the traditional ring of choice. Even though diamonds are beautiful, there are other less expensive alternatives. If we are saving for a down payment for a home, furniture, or other expenditures, settle for a gold band. There will be future anniversaries where a surprise diamond ring can be given. In the meantime, it's a joint decision of saving money for a worthwhile cause. It could set the tone for money smarts for the rest of our lives. It is not written in stone that only a diamond is given as a wedding ring. However, through media advertising, the DeBeers diamond family would want you to think otherwise.

Discuss if both of us want children, and how many. It costs money to raise children. Figure out, according to income and budget how many children can easily be raised. Take into account the monies spent from pregnancy through college. There are pros and cons here: sacrifices and retirement funds. If financial stress becomes part of the stage of raising a larger family, maybe, instead of having many children, a few less would suffice. The children will reap the financial benefits to help secure their future. I'm not advocating that parents deprive themselves of a large family, but I am saying, be aware of our financial circumstances first.

And will both parents be content with the choices about having children? Are we both in harmony with a savings plan? Are the savings accounts to be joint or individual? What are our feelings about saving for college for our children? Are we both willing to take an active role in the children's studies?

The more monetary subjects that are discussed prior to marriage, the less discord there'll be later.

If we are intimidated by our partner-to-be concerning their ideas on finances, tell them how we feel. Maybe the one doing the intimidating doesn't realize they are doing it. Explain how low it makes us feel now, and how we would like to feel later if they stop pressuring us. If the coercion continues, think hard. If we were treated this way before marriage, would we want to spend the rest of our life with that person? We need to come to a mutual understanding before marriage. If not, walk.

Do we agree on vehicles before marriage? Does one person want a splashy expensive one, while the other is satisfied with a less expensive one? We need to realize if we want a family, it's probably better to have the less expensive vehicle. Another point is having a self-entitled attitude and little money to back it up: "I can afford it, so what's the problem?" "I don't care. This is what I want." In our present economy, many people are being laid off, even those who thought their jobs and pensions were secure. What would happen to our family and expenses if this happened to us? Would we have to refinance the car, take a second mortgage, or lose both? If more people realized a vehicle is just a way to get from one point to another, then what purpose does it serve to own one that's expensive and flashy? Aren't the long-term goals more important? Is having the newest, the best, or most expensive tangibles worth trading our security? One thing is for sure. There is no price on irreplaceable intangibles that a secure family life offers.

In conclusion: Decide before marriage how every possible monetary decision is to be handled. Through open communication and maintenance of PAA, the financial aspects of marriage should go smoothly.

MARRIAGE

After marriage, situations can change. Financial adjustments and modifications need to be reached amiably through compromise. Act as a team. When children see parents at odds concerning money, they will become confused and frustrated, leading them into a future of financial instability.

When we use the pre-marriage section and positive attitude adjustment as a financial guide throughout our marriage, and have an ongoing, open repartee concerning money matters, we set a healthy life stage for many years to come.

DIVORCE

It's true that when we first marry we presume ours will last a lifetime, although we know that a good percentage end in divorce. How does this happen?

One way to help reduce the possibility of divorce in our life is to discuss every feeling, every possible scenario of life that we can possibly think of before marriage. The high quality of conversation and communication should continue throughout our marriage. Each of us has our own lifestyles, feelings, and idiosyncrasies. Come to a mutual agreement on everything imaginable. As new topics arise, we will already have the know-how to communicate and come to amicable solutions. I speak through experience that sarcasm, belittling, screaming, and attacking the person instead of the deed, should not be an option.

PAA must be exercised to the fullest, being that monetary and emotional stresses are so high.

It's true, however, that sometimes divorce is the only option. Here again, PAA should step in to lead us into a new chapter of our life.

SINGLE LIVING

Single living, as in all other kinds of lifestyles, brings its own rewards and downfalls.

No matter how people choose to live, PAA is an invaluable companion for financial security.

I've lived singly and have seen how others live as singles. They may choose to do so or may be rebuilding a life after divorce or loss of a spouse, or simply be in the lower income bracket; consequently, many singles decide to share living facilities until they are able to "go it alone." They share rent and utilities, cutting their expenses in half.

Before we go out on our own for the first time, we need to plan ahead. Make sure we have enough money put aside to cover first and last months rent, plus a security deposit, money to turn on utilities, and enough saved to cover unexpected contingencies.

Women that find themselves alone for the first time often find finances perplexing, especially if they have never had to balance a checkbook or live frugally. No matter if we are single, married, or in a relationship, we owe it to us to learn positive attitude adjustment. We need to be financially aware so we are able to handle any economic contingency.

People that have better earning capabilities have the world at their doorstep. Since they have no money problems, they can spend or save at their discretion. However, PAA plays its role here, as well. They still need to be prudent, live beneath their income, having savings and a retirement account, be responsible with credit cards and respond intelligently to the great American marketing machine.

EMPTY NEST

By this time in our life, we should be extra cognizant of handling finances. By following PAA, there should enough put away for old age security, *BUT…*

There could be a huge downfall here, if we have allowed outside forces to bleed those funds into oblivion. One or more of our children may want to "borrow" money from us. The reasons vary drastically. It may be to start a business, a down payment on a home, flying to see them when emergencies arise, or to get them out of self-inflicted financial debt, and even to pay for their prescriptions. The list is endless.

If parents bow down time and again to help adult children, and if they don't make an effort to repay, our retirement funds can easily dwindle down to nothing.

A customer at the bank I worked for had a daughter who was on drugs. When the customer, a widow, first opened her account she had sufficient retirement income. When her daughter *needed* money, she would withdraw from her retirement account to help her. Over a few years, I watched as the mother's account was bled dry.

Scenario: Grandmother and grown daughter are both widowed and left with enough funds to live comfortably throughout the rest of their lives. The daughter has four grown children. Enter grandchild number one, who wants to start a business. Between inventory and the building, the cost runs into several hundred thousand dollars. The mother, thinking it's a good investment, gives the child the money. The business goes belly up. The mother is out her money. How can the mother help one child without helping the others? She finds herself in a domino effect, helping her other children as well. As the mother's funds diminish, the grandmother steps in and before they know it, both their nest eggs are gone!

Don't let this happen to us! Forewarned is forearmed.

This scenario may not have happened in the first place if the family had been exposed to PAA beforehand.

But then, there are conscientious young adults who may have borrowed small sums of money from parents but have diligently repaid the loans. If the young adults do show integrity and prove that they are trustworthy, it's easier to loan money for emergencies in the future. If they do not repay a loan in good faith, one loan is enough. They're on their own!

I believe that giving money to adult children (other than for dire emergencies) weakens their ability to stand on their own feet. If they don't work for something, they esteem it lightly, but if they do work hard for things, they will value them more.

A favorite fun pastime for grandparents is spoiling grandchildren. Every time they see them they give them a present, and the cost eats away at retirement funds. PAA warns against this practice for another reason. Children start to expect gifts, therefore, leading to self-entitlement mindsets.

During the empty nest years, frugality should be the norm, unless there are no money worries at all. When grown children are on their own, the extra income not spent supporting them should be invested toward retirement, not spent frivolously or for bailing them out.

Scenario 1: There are people who cast aside the idea of retirement accounts. They have no clue of PAA. Then, when they reach their 50s, all of a frantic sudden, the retirement idea hits them! Their credit card debt may take years to pay off. Prices are always on the rise. A job is lost. Panic sets in and for good reason.

Scenario 2: These same people, if fortified with PAA, would have started a retirement plan early on, even though "the golden years" seemed a lifetime away.

RETIREMENT

This last life cycle brings it all home to rest.

Either we have been astute or lackadaisical in putting money aside for retirement. It's us who must face the financial consequences or the well-being of our retirement.

I'm not discounting those of us who have been thrust into a lesser lifestyle by accidents, illnesses, tragedies, or by being victims of crime, handicap, disabilities, or other serious situations.

I am saying that we who have had a choice, had PAA knowledge, and still chose the wrong financial path, need to be prepared for a rude awakening.

By this time in our life, it's too late to go back to being more prudent. The dye has been cast. Working in a retired community for 19 years, I saw this happen too many times. That's why it's so important to learn PAA at an early age and allow it to be our companion throughout our life cycle. Remember — positive attitude adjustment is our life preserver, which is essential when we are living on a fixed income.

Many of us may flounder in confusion when it comes to planning our retirement because we do not have the knowledge to accomplish this multifaceted task.

The U.S. Department of Labor has printed a publication that I ordered through Parade Magazine from Sunny Pueblo Home of the Federal Citizen Information Center called "Taking the Mystery out of Retirement." It's a comprehensive compilation of everything we need to know to intelligently plan our retirement from A to Z. To order a copy, visit www.pueblo.gsa.gov

It's not only the well to do that live comfortably in retirement. Almost anyone who has learned the secrets of PAA can also live well in old age: maybe without all the frills as the wealthy, but still comfortable.

Take advantage of senior discounts. Always ask for them wherever we are. Businesses can offer them but may not advertise them.

Boredom sometimes hits the retiree. Having a job, even a part-time job can ease monotony and money stresses as well. Not only will it make us feel better, it also gives a hedge against inflation, a hedge against fluctuating interest rates, or downward spirals in the stock market.

Scenario: Before PAA, throughout Widdley's working years, he paid little attention to retirement. His priorities were lavishing gifts onto family, going on expensive vacations, purchasing high priced jewelry, and buying other extravagances. Now it's time to retire and his vehicle has over 100,000 miles. All of a sudden he wonders where the money will come from to replace it.

All the rationalizations and excuses for spending that Widdley used during his productive income years will come to haunt him. He thought he had everything planned out, but he rationalized the reality.

Every purchase made or not made during working years will make retirement easier or more difficult.

Scenario after PAA: All the clothes not purchased, all the times we said "It's only money" not spent, all the times we've lived below our means, and all the self-entitlements not practiced, add up over a lifetime, and are enough to finance a replacement vehicle during retirement.

When we take early retirement and receive the funds in one lump sum, we need to be extra prudent in investing it so as to give us the best return for our money. We may feel wealthy with all this newfound money and think it will not matter much if we pay for college tuitions or set our children up in a business. Do not get caught in this financial nightmare. Children can work part time to pay college expenses and they can go to a bank to borrow money to start a business. Once our retirement funds are gone, there's no way to replace it.

CHAPTER RECAP

Positive attitude adjustment teachings should begin at the earliest possible age. Children will incorporate it into their lives so slowly that it will be ingrained for life by the time they are half grown.

Parents should play a huge part in guiding children toward financial fitness, which is just as important as teaching them reading, writing and math. They should act as a strong unit and be good role models.

We all need to go back to the basic ideals of family life that enhance saving money, not encourage spending money irresponsibly. Not only do we need to teach PAA, but to show tangible lessons of it as well. Give children consistent financial structure throughout their growing years, so as teens, they will already be responsible money managers.

Avoid family finance secrets. Let our children hear us mention in passing, “Now that credit card is paid in full.” Let them hear us discussing retirement planning and why we choose to live simply.

During the dating years there are choices to be made. Decide, before hand, how much and where to spend money, and still have a good time.

It’s important that young adults and college students realize the serious responsibility of credit cards.

Make amiable financial decisions before marriage. It sets the pace for lifelong strategies.

Even a wedding can be moderate. An expensive wedding and reception does not guarantee a blissful life.

It’s never too early to begin retirement accounts.

From marriage until retirement, we need to be prudent, protecting our finances, because we may have huge medical expenses in later years, and assisted living facilities and nursing homes are not cheap.

In retirement or otherwise, do not fall into the trap of bailing out our adult children. They need to be economically independent. By assisting them our own old age savings could rapidly disappear. And it could also cripple the child's ability of become financially astute.

CHAPTER 9

BOOKS

So we want to read a new book that's just come out? We could be tempted to buy the hard cover for premium price like we used to or now wait for the paperback, which saves money. Cheaper yet, free in fact, check it out at the library!

However, some books are worth purchasing. Those that have information we wish to refer back to from time to time, such as *A Life Preserver in a Sea of Debt*, which will keep us on the path to permanent financial astuteness.

I had wanted some recipes from a cookbook that cost $28. I didn't want to spend that much. In fact, I didn't want to spend anything. I checked the cookbook out of the library, and copied the recipes by hand. Free. Having them copied at a copy store would have been $4.10, still a far cry from $28. Copying them on a computer or ordering online are other options.

Secondhand bookstores offer used paperbacks and hard covers at discounts. They make deals. Buying more than one can reap discounts. Having books to sell to the bookstore can get us more discounts. Return the book to the store and get a discount on our next purchase. The library is cheaper still, but the books must be returned by a specific date.

Every time we use the library to read a book instead of purchasing it, put the money aside that we would have spent. How much could be saved in a year?

College bound? Buy used books from other students or from the college bookstore or pawnshops!

Many friends and relatives' homes have large libraries. Try a mutual lending agreement. Think of all the books available. The prerequisite here is having the respect to return them in a timely fashion.

E-books or electronic books are available through library systems. This service is free and books can be checked out 24 hours a day from anywhere. First we need to visit a library, set up an account, obtain a card, a password, user name, and have access to a computer. Then go on the library's web site, click on Ebooks and continue from there. Books are checked out and have return dates like regular books, only we use computers to read them, not the book itself. E-books offer several aspects that regular books do not have. We can key in a word or phrase and find it anywhere in the book and the type size can be adjusted to large print. A handy dictionary enables us to look up unfamiliar words immediately.

Purchasing books online is yet another avenue of saving money.

CHAPTER 10

SPENDING AND SAVING

This chapter explains how spending and saving are intertwined. When practiced with PAA they have a symbiotic relationship that produces permanent economic stability. Wayne von Borstel, a financial planner, said "Money is a drug, the #1 drug in America. It gives us a quick high every time we spend it. If we have a good day, we spend money. If we have a bad day, we spend money. It makes us feel good." We have become addicted to spending.

We are spoiled. We're used to tasting everything our great country offers. This attitude has been built into our culture. We want newer versions, the latest fashions, we want the advertised bigger and better, and the list goes on. We take it for granted. It's owed to us. We deserve it. Albertson's Supermarket, Macy's Department Store, and Cardinal True Value Hardware have thousands of products. That doesn't mean we have to buy one of everything or the newest gizmo. This attitude should be with us in any place that sells merchandise. Reprogram our mindsets. We should buy only those items that we need. Have a list and stick to it.

Yes. We have the luxury of freedom. We have the privilege of the newest technologies. This does not mean we should buy things just because they are available, the Jones's have one, or a friend recommends it. We have made some of these mistakes in the past, but now we are more discerning. We will not be swayed anymore. We know our self-gratification is better served by paying bills as opposed to buy-a-holic habits that slip us further into debt.

Buying deletes assets. Saving increases assets.

In order to reach optimal financial stability we need to know the difference between a need and a want so we may spend or save accordingly. "Needs" are what we need to survive, like food and shelter, and "wants" are the extras that can bring us an inflated sense of self-gratification. It's up to us to choose. We either benefit from knowing the difference between the two or we remain in debt. John has always kept needs and wants separate and nothing ever persuaded him to do otherwise. This is another avenue to grab the life preserver.

1. John never assumes anything, including money matters. He checks, double checks and he compares again. There may be two 12-ounce bottles for less than one 24-ounce bottle. True, it's usually the other way around. He compares prices anyway.
2. Stores often prominently display higher priced merchandise in the front where shopper traffic is heaviest. We looked at water containers in the Army Navy store priced at $36 at the front of the store. In the back, hidden from view and tucked in a corner, we found the same size container for $10.00.
3. Instant gratifications and purchasing wants put us in the poorhouse. Before adopting PAA, compulsive shopping relieved our stress. For instance: We attend all four arts and crafts shows in our area. At each show we spend $30 on incidentals. If we do not have a nest egg

or we owe someone money, the $120 would have been more wisely spent or saved.

4. Why do stores have so much merchandise to look at right next to the checkout stands? There is good reason for this. The stores try to impose sneaky tactics to weasel more money from us where we are least expecting it. And what better place to do it when we are stuck in line, wiling away our time, scanning the magazines, candy, and other merchandise? Before we know it some of these items are in our carts. And we had no intention of purchasing them when we went into the store!

Media entices us to spend money at every turn. Instant gratification syndrome oozes into every niche and cranny. We see *it*. We want *it*. There's a 1-800 number! WOW! We feel our adrenaline pumping. We call and order *it*, with no thought of the shipping and handling charges, or that the same item could be easily found in a discount store near us.

Instant gratification does one thing. It provides us with an easy road to debt. Before PAA, compulsive shopping relieved our stress. After PAA, we address reasons for our stress, pinpoint them, decide on a solution to eliminate them, and then act on that solution. We also ask ourselves what the consequences are if we spend money; if it diminishes our ability to pay for future prescriptions or an insurance policy.

Instead of buying a huge TV for over $5,000, buy a smaller one, and make an IRA contribution or invest in property with the difference.

We may think we want something so much we rationalize that it is a need and we cannot live without it.

Stop! Think! Do not buy on impulse. Practice positive attitude adjustment. The money is still ours, and chances are, later on, we won't even remember what it was that we chose not to purchase.

Would thinking about every buying decision ruin our day? Turn pessimistic attitudes into positive ones. We are glad to save money. PAA is proud we are making good progress.

My instant gratification scenario: I went shopping and spotted a gorgeous small, decorated storage chest. I just couldn't leave it in the store. I really wanted it. I could feel the excitement! "ARRGH!" cried PAA. I stepped back to reevaluate the situation. "I do love it, but…I have no room for it and I'd need to buy a stand for it." I left the store empty handed, chuckling under my breath. Thanks PAA. I still have my money.

"Oh, it's only $1.50; it's only $3.99." "I have a little extra money. What's the harm?" There's plenty of harm. Every time we say "it's only" think of that much money saved by not buying it. If we had bought it, think of it as money thrown into the garbage. Once it's there, it's gone forever. By not buying every time we see something we want, the money saved really adds up.

If we keep spending money using these rationalizations, "the lunch is only $6.99", "the picture frame is only $9.99", "the hammer is only $29", and a few days later it's something else, the debt cycle continues. At the end of the month we have spent over $100 not included in our budget. It's even worse if we have charged the purchases. There's interest to pay as well. It's no wonder we find ourselves muttering, "We never have enough money."

No matter what the rationalization is to buy, this hard fact remains; the money spent on the purchase is gone for good.

Haggling is a diplomatic way of trying to purchase something for less than the asking price. Some people frown on this practice, think it's cheap and unworthy behavior. But there are some of us who make it a part of our PAA. It never hurts to ask for a lower price. The worst scenario is they say "no." But some do say "yes."

For those who choose not to haggle, that's fine. But what I am saying is that if we do bargain, there's a proper way of doing it.

Scenario: John and I had a $1,000 budget for a new sofa. We came across one on sale for $1,150 reduced from $1,495. Respectfully, tactfully and courteously, we explained our budget to the salesperson. She excused herself to confer with management to see if it was possible to meet our figure. We did this twice at two separate stores. Our price was met once and the other item was only $50 more instead of $200 more.

Scenario: John and I purchased five gallons of paint on sale. It was not enough. We returned to the store to buy more, but the sale had ended. I glanced at my watch and said to the salesman, very diplomatically, "Um…it's 3:17 P.M. on the second Tuesday of the month and one lucky customer is to receive an expired sale item at the sale price." In Sherwin Williams, no one had ever heard that before and the salesman was quite taken aback by the good humor. We not only got the sale price but an extra 10% discount. My husband was amazed. If I hadn't used a humorous tale, maybe we wouldn't have gotten the sale price. The store, by exercising good customer relations, knew they'd have a repeat customer. After that incident, whenever we've needed paint, we have returned to Sherwin Williams, but always taking advantage of sales.

As exhilarating a story as the Sherman Williams experience was, here is a negative comparison: For 16 years we had shopped at a health food store. Several years ago, the quality of customer service declined. They had said in previous years, if a product had not been in stock, they'd be happy to get it. Now, pointing to another product, they retorted, "This is the only one we carry." The bottom fell out when we wanted a sale item toward the end of the sale. The owner said he could not order it for the sale price anymore; if we still wanted the item, we would have to pay retail price. Technically, the vegetable burgers were on sale three more days. Well, that was the end of our patronage to that store. I have found out since then, that other customers have been treated like I was. Other health food stores in our area bend over backwards to satisfy customer's needs, which includes helping them save money.

Lesson: If a store doesn't want to honor sales, go elsewhere. Sherwin Williams has gained thousands of dollars from our repeat patronage while the health food store will lose thousands of dollars by their poor customer relations.

Scenario: We needed a freezer and a box store had one for $495, cash or credit card. The same freezer at a discount showroom was $549. We politely asked if they would meet the box store's price. The discount showroom met the price, gave us 90 days interest free to pay for it, and they delivered it free of charge. The box store didn't have delivery service. We saved in more ways than one. Receiving 90 days interest free, same as cash, was easier on our budget.

Scenario: Needing to purchase silk flowers to make an arrangement, I came across packaged bags of flowers for $9.99 apiece. Each bag had too many for my needs. I politely asked if I could have half of two packages. The salesperson cheerfully complied. Instead of spending $19.99, the bill was $9.99. I saved 50% and got exactly what I needed.

In one day, John and I saved this amount of money by comparing prices:

1. Cone tips for a hiking stick: Specialty store: $5.95, Wal-Mart: $1.95.
2. New Alternator for truck at Ford Dealership: $375, at our favorite vehicle mechanic: $235.
3. 8 pack batteries at Shopko: $4.50, other stores' lowest price: $6.45. Our total savings was $145.95!

Rental storage unit businesses are thriving. Their owners have caught on to our bandwagon of overindulgence. We buy so much '*stuff*' we do not '*need*' we must pay to store it. Positive attitude adjustment goes into a ludicrous tantrum. Sell, give away, or donate our excesses. Save the monthly storage fees. However, at times, we may need a storage facility; for instance, between moves, or for other short-term use. But to pay for storing our overabundance of '*stuff*' that we bought and do not use interferes with our financial goals.

If we have unexpected bills and need to purchase a high end product, tell the salesperson. Usually, they'll be able to help us. They'll know that when we have better times, we will be repeat customers.

When buying many items, suggest an across the board discount or throw in a few extra bonuses. For instance, if we are redesigning our yard and garden, we need fencing, weed guard fabric, hoses, bird feeder, a hoe, shovel, garden tools, benches, lumber, paint, and other things. However, we won't get a discount if we don't ask.

Garage Sales: Know prices of new items before buying anything used. Take into consideration how old it is, and how much it will be used. Buy things we need, not outlandish oddities that will end up in the garbage. By taking PAA to garage sales it'll help us make the best decisions at the prices we can afford. But before spending money on anything, think about how to buy it for less.

Sales: An item goes on sale. Watch out. Know our prices. Do math. Examples:

1. An aspirin product is 30 count for $8.99. Another store has the same product, 40 count for the same price.
2. A video store tape sale is three tapes for $6.00. Another store sells a nine pack for $14.99.

Scenario: I saw a shirt at the mall for $100 and the same shirt at a discount mall for $45. I bought the discount shirt and saved over 50%. I knew this shirt would get a lot of wear.

However, some special sales include merchandise that has been brought in exclusively for that sale. It is not from regular stock. It can be a lower quality than regular stock. I saw a sweatshirt on sale at my favorite department store. The regular price was $40, on sale for $24. There was no way the sweatshirt was worth $40 and no way that it was this store's original merchandise. It was inferior quality, and made of a thin fabric. This was definitely an item that was brought into the store exclusively for the sale. Know merchandise. Don't be taken in just because an item is on sale.

Sometimes formal stationery needs to be used for specific occasions. This is fine. But what about all the other times we like to casually touch base with others? Enter PAA. Use notebook paper, plain white paper, legal pads, colored paper pads or hand-decorated paper instead of expensive boxed stationery, which "it's only" $8.99 or $10.99. The words in the letter mean the same to the recipient whether it's written on plain or fancy paper. Packaged note cards, likewise, cost a lot of money. Cut 8X10 paper in half, and buy plain envelopes to fit and we are in good shape. Hand-decorate the card and envelope.

Do we see something new in a department store that we would love to buy? We know better than to pay full retail. When I worked at Macy's as a second job I learned a few tricks. Consider waiting a few days or a week or so. Check back with the store. It may have gone on sale. So, we go back and it's nowhere to be found. Ask! It may be in the back, waiting to be marked down for a sale. The more questions we ask, the more likely we will save money.

Perfumes and Aftershave Lotions: PAA reality check! Sure the aroma of perfumes and lotions delight the senses. They are enjoyable to wear. It's fun whiffing different brands and deciding which one is special for us. Is it also fun to lay out lavish sums to please our desire to "temporarily smell good?" Showering washes aromas off and the purchase money goes down the drain. Of course, the decision is ours. If we wear perfumes and use scented lotions, we only derive several hours of pleasure before the fragrance is gone. We have either thrown money away or saved it. Other people don't like us any more or less because of how we smell. They like us for us.

For back pain, we can buy a $25 packet with Velcro closures. We insert an ice pack into a pocket that's included with the packet. Then we place the ice packet over the pain area and secure it around our waist with the Velcro straps. This gives us mobility to walk around while getting relief. After learning positive attitude adjustment, we make a packet from old sheets and buy Velcro for a dollar. The ice pack can come from a picnic cooler or a package of frozen peas.

It's smart to stock up on essentials while they're on sale. However, keep the purchases in line with our budget.

Author's scenario: I used to go overboard buying items on sale to the point that I ran out of money before the end of the week! I saved so much, I almost ended up in the poorhouse and some of the item's expiration dates ran out before I could use the product.

We needed a new doormat. We bought one at a Dollar Store. It had deep pile that was perfect for brushing dirt from shoes, and it was washable. Or we could have gone directly to a carpet store and asked for a discontinued sample. We have also seen carpet stores throwing away carpet remnants, enough for 10 floor mats.

Author's scenario: We were dumping our garbage at a collection site and a woman was throwing away an entire household of merchandise! There had been a death in the family. We went home with oodles of perfectly good merchandise. The woman was happy we took some. What we didn't use ourselves, we sold at a garage sale.

Jewelry: Sure it's nice to own. It's beautiful. It enhances outfits. It can be worn as an ego feeder. It can be worn to outdo others. It can be purchased in as many colors as you have clothing. It can be a status symbol. It's fun to buy and wear. Just imagine PAA's reaction if it peered into our jewelry box! Jewelry can also be conservatively purchased in a few basic colors that will go well with anything you wear. The money saved could pay for emergencies in the future.

Frivolity Purchases: Fireworks. Yes, they are fun and quite beautiful. We have pros and cons here too. We could buy them every year, experience excitement, and literally watch our money go up in flames. No pun intended. Or…after PAA, we realize we have a choice. We can cut back. Decide to either purchase half the amount or buy them every other year or two. At least it won't seem as if the smoke and flames are so thick with our money burning away in the nighttime breezes. Another choice is being content watching others setting off their fireworks and enjoying the sparkling phenomenon while keeping our money intact.

Cutting back on nonessentials gives us extra money for essentials. Remember wants versus needs and rationalization versus realization.

There are many of us who have hidden expenditures from a loved one. I am not speaking about spending into bankruptcy. I am speaking about everyday, normal purchases. Every so often we need to treat ourselves. This is okay, but think of the consequences of hiding purchases in other instances. To have a healthy financial atmosphere in our home there needs to be openness, understanding, truthfulness and support. Sometimes, where there are two voices communicating, money could be saved or spent in other important areas where both parties will benefit instead of just one. Then, at other times, the expenditure should be supported and praised by the other party. Whatever our choice, it's healthier to bring things out in the open than it is hiding it. Financially, we both benefit.

Writing down dreams, wishes, and wants is a constructive activity. Carry these things in our mind whenever we are about to spend money. It's a sure way to keep rationalization from overpowering realization. Temptation to buy fizzles like an old carbonated soda.

Say we buy lunch five days a week for "it's only" \$5.00 a day. That's "it's only" \$25 a week, "it's only" \$100 a month, "it's only" \$1,200 a year. For "it's only" \$20 a month, we could have bought lunch ingredients from the supermarket and made our lunches. Presto! We save \$80 a month, \$960 a year, with just "it's only". Over a 40-year working career we will have saved over \$38,400. Keep a record of all the "it's only" amounts of dollar expenditures we could spend money on, for a month, but don't. At the month's end, add up all the "it's only" and see how much we have saved.

My daughter-in-law, Kelly, adds this to saving on "it's only." Save and reward at the same time. Physically put aside all the money saved by saying *no* to items by practicing PAA. Then, each month, count out the money, take a preset percentage and spend it on whatever we want. No secrets, just earned fun money. Save the rest since it would have previously been wasted prior to PAA. It will not be missed. When we need that house, car, piano, or whatever, the money will be there.

Trade: Yes, like in the good old days. Trade our bulk garden vegetables for other garden goodies we don't grow. Do we sew, but not drive? Trade! Are we a carpenter but not a vehicle mechanic? Trade! Presto! No money spent, and we get what we need.

Do we have fixed monthly payments? Pay a little more each month, thereby paying down the principal, and at the same time, saving on interest charged.

Did we receive a raise? Pretend we didn't. Save every penny and watch it grow. If we did get a raise, it means we worked very hard for it, and it shouldn't be thrown out for nonessentials. If we don't have enough money to contribute to our IRA this year, use our raise money.

We save all paper we receive as junk mail that is blank on one side. We cut or rip the papers in sections and use them as scratch paper. We haven't bought scratch pads in 20 years!

If bulk size packages, which are cheaper, are too large for our family to use up or our storage space is limited, split the package and the cost with a friend or neighbor. We save on the bulk rate and we have the exact amount that we want.

John does our own lawn work, repairs and painting. He never hires these jobs out unless he has exhausted all other possibilities. A lawn maintenance man wanted $400 to get our property cleaned up from the winter. John did it himself even though his shoulders are arthritic. A fence company wanted $8,000 to replace our rotting log fence. Even though it was back breaking work, John took his time and did it himself.

We have high windows that need cleaning once a year. The professionals wanted $400. Again, John took his time and cleaned them himself. The outside logs of our home need scrubbing down in the spring. Instead of paying to have it done, John rents a pressure cleaner and does it himself. Every five years the logs need to be repainted. This entails three coats for which professionals charge several thousand dollars. John did it himself. No wonder we have such a nice savings account.

We always take refunds and rebate checks and any loose change directly to the savings account, no matter how small or large the amount.

Stores usually take inventories twice a year, in January and July. Check our favorite stores for both pre and post inventory sales. Savings are huge. One or two day sales also offer big savings.

Prioritize. Figure out what's most important to us. Saving, spending, staying debt-free, and should I, or shouldn't I convert to PAA?

Double up with friends or neighbors on the costs of newspapers, magazines, and sending multiple bills in one envelope. This is not being a cheapskate. It's being frugal and money conscious.

Leave our checkbook, credit and debit cards at home when we go shopping. Take only the amount of cash we wish to spend.

Be selective. Compare. Do we see something we would like to buy? Walk away from it. Think of all the aspects. Then go back and see if it's still important enough to spend money on.

I've lived my entire life without it. Do I really *need* it now?

Save at the beginning of a pay period. Be conservative so we will not be caught short. Then, after a month of PAA, see how much more money is left over at the end of the pay period. Instead of the old scared feeling that we have overspent and don't have the funds for basics, we find ourselves at ease. We have unraveled the secret!

We have changed our mindset. We are now managing our money to full advantage.

Catalogs. Do we receive numerous mail order catalogs? Do we have a few favorites? Do we finger through all of them and order products we normally wouldn't use? Keep only our favorites. Call the other catalog companies' 1-800 numbers and request they take us off their mailing list.

Before ordering from any catalog, compare shipping and handling charges. From the catalogs we receive, the charges vary from $3.50 to $8.45 for a $35 order. One big name company charges a $3.00 fee above and beyond shipping and handling per order! Yes, some companies are arrogant that way. We cancelled the catalog. A competitor offers free shipping when we use their credit card. That company has the same merchandise value. The result is clear. The free shipping and handling company gets all our business. So what if it does have a different label? The quality of the goods is the same.

Some shipping and handling charges are predicated on weight; others offer a flat fee. Go through several catalogs, being aware of these differences. There are pros and cons here. But now we have the knowledge to make the best choice.

Catalogs have end of season sales. There are good buys. We can save a lot of money.

Sometimes a similar item to that in a catalog can be found in a local store. It's equivalent to the catalog product, for less than the catalog price. Know quality and prices.

Go shopping for the day with others who are in the same financial bracket as us. We will have fun comparing and saving money. We will spend less than if we had gone shopping with people in a higher income bracket.

Beauty Salons and Barber Shops: Women's hair color and weaves are about $45 here. Permanents are $42 and up. Tanning is $25. Haircuts are $18. Men's shaves are

$10, hair color is $25, a manicure is $15, and a beard trim is $4. Figure out how much we spend on these items in a year. Is the cost worth the money not saved? Weigh this against a simpler hairstyle, our vanity, and money saved. Extend haircuts an extra week or color our own hair.

Hanging folders. A package of 10 in one store is $6.69. Another store has the same package for $3.77. Know our prices. If we weren't aware that $6.69 was priced too high, we may have purchased them.

What else could be done besides going on a shopping spree to get out of the doldrums or depression (which would certainly elevate credit card balances)? What else gives the same high level of importance? The quickest way to talk ourselves out of going shopping to kill boredom is to go over our financial goals. See how close we are to our vacation, to the college fund, or to paying off debts. Then, instead of going shopping, we put the money to better use elsewhere. We settle down to a hobby, go for a brisk walk or jog, or catch up on correspondence. Also we could go to garage sales with a money limit or dig into a long laid-off project.

When buying anything, think how long it will be used. Is it a fad or something used only a short time, or does it have long-term usage? Buying fads and short-term usage items is throwing money away.

If someone swears to us that a particular thought or product is the best and most truthful, do our own research. What's best for one may not be best for us. They may be trying to pull the wool over our eyes for personal gain, jealousy, or revenge. A friend may go into business and try to pressure us into buying what they are selling. Because of the friendship they will think they have an edge: an easy sale. Only after careful thought and consideration, make up our mind. We shouldn't have to cower down and be pulled into anything we don't want.

If we knew we would have to discard an item to make room for the new, would we still purchase it?

Say, we are looking to buy a certain product. In the store are several different ones to choose from, ranging from inexpensive, moderately priced, a little more expensive, and the top of the line. What would we do? Think how long it will be used and how often. Many would choose the medium priced product. However, don't be fooled. Read what each one has to offer. Compare and regroup. Don't take anything for granted. Then make a decision.

Triumph over wise and thought out financial decisions.

However, the best made plans can go awry due to outside forces. If this happens to us, will we charge, withdraw from our IRA, or will we get a second job until our finances even out? Don't wait until time runs out.

Instead of buy, buy, buy, save and invest. No matter what others do or we have done in the past, we can use positive attitude adjustment from here on. Be strong. Learn to say no and mean it.

No matter what we think we are owed (self-gratification), our first priority is to stay debt-free.

Compare overspending to overeating. Each one is detrimental — one to our finances, the other to our health. Practicing positive attitude adjustment will help us not to succumb to the temptations of either.

When shopping, if we say, "Just one more thing I have to buy", think instead, "Just one more thing I can enter in my book of things wanted but not bought!" Saved and not spent.

Remember to use coupons. Remember to mail in rebates. Remember to file receipts. I used to forget about coupons in my purse. Now I paper clip them to my list. I keep the rebate with the receipt. Before filing the receipt, the reminder of the rebate is right there. Yes, I file every receipt. We were robbed once and many articles were taken. The insurance company requested receipts of the stolen goods. I had them all.

Realizing, not rationalizing, if the more expensive product is the most cost-effective in the long run, go for it. If the least expensive product is easier or more comfortable, go for that one. There are choices, pros and cons, thoughts and decisions. Make the best of them. Be cognizant of our financial status at all times. Update when necessary. Be aware of how much money is going out and how much money is coming in. If the two allow no margin, reevaluate the situation and decide how to spend more wisely, and how to further cut back. This should be done on a regular basis so as not to fall into a debt pattern.

Be aware of choices and our surroundings. Are others near us making multiple purchases? Are we in a more expensive store than our budget allows? Is there loud exciting music that's hyping us into a buying frenzy? Is there a sale we just can't miss?

Shopaholics may wonder why their retirement funds aren't worth more, or why they seem to always be in debt. Once they adopt PAA, they will have answers.

I could never understand why people spend money on to-go foods or eat out when they have unpaid bills. Even if the cost of these foods is not enough to pay the bills in full, every penny helps.

Socks: Buy in one color. If one gets worn out, pair it with another.

Every time we save money, it is better in our pocket than someone else's pocket.

There's hardly a time when John buys a "want" for himself. If he "needs" a specific item, he goes into a store and buys only that item. He is not swayed to buy more. This is one of his secrets of being financially astute.

Photo album sale: "It's only $10.00." Now I can put all my pictures away. Stop! Go to a dollar store and purchase two $1 00.photo boxes. We save $8.00. Or better yet, pick up several empty boxes from a gift shop or supermarket and decorate them. Our savings are $10.00!

Be cognizant of the consequences of spending money. Spend it constructively, not irresponsibly. Focus! Be accountable. We benefit!

Money saving tips:

1. Use less of everything
2. Buy generics
3. Drive less
4. Stay home instead of going shopping
5. Be aware of expiration dates
6. Never equate possessions with happiness
7. Keep from getting so caught up in the moment that consequences are forgotten.

Avoid:

1. Library fines
2. Late fees for returning rentals
3. Paying bills late
4. Falling behind on vehicle maintenance
5. Buying excessive amounts of food (less is thrown out)
6. Buying items that are never used
7. Shopping on line for items we wouldn't normally buy
8. Feeding our instant gratification when we purchase munchies from snack bars

CHAPTER 11

CHRISTMAS, GIFTS AND OTHER HOLIDAYS

John never went over his budget to buy gifts for any occasion. Sometimes I thought him a tightwad, but he always knew our financial circumstances and spent accordingly. So how could I get upset with him when he was looking out for our best interest? The broader picture always took precedence over self-satisfaction purchases. This is another area that helps us transition.

Birthday, anniversary, engagement, wedding, and graduation gifts are associated with spending money. And do not forget the cards, wrapping paper, and mailing costs. Each one of these expenditures can be reduced. Think of our overall picture of future goals. Compare prices of gifts from several stores to get the best deal. If we cut our gift budget across the board, we can still buy appropriate presents.

Aah, but then there's the Christmas Bonus…the mere joy of the words imply it's ours to freely spend. But positive attitude adjustment recommends budgeting holiday expenditures. Save the entire bonus and pay holiday costs out of ready cash or save half of the bonus and wisely spend the rest. So how do we know which decision to make? Do we have outstanding bills? Will our tires need replacing in the near future? Do we have a life insurance premium coming due, or are we saving money for a honeymoon, or a house down payment? Only we can decide which is more important to spend our Christmas bonus.

The holiday season bombards us with thousands of gift choices. Everywhere we go, the *buy, buy, buy* syndrome presents itself through the enticements of ads, mega decorations in every niche and cranny, and sales that are too good to be true. This atmosphere has been present all of our lives, but it used to start later in the year. In the 1950s, the Friday after Thanksgiving would herald in the holiday shopping season. Now we see the holiday shopping season pushed further back, first to October before we got a chance to celebrate Halloween, and now holiday decorations are in stores as early as September! No matter when we see the first signs of Christmas; we automatically respond to the signal like the starting shot in a sprint.

Media can and does control our thinking, behavior, and purchasing habits "if" we are not made aware of their ploys. Know what we can afford, make lists accordingly, and stay within our budget. Remember *not to overspend in just one area* and then *another.*

Ads tell us where to go after Christmas to help pay our holiday debts. "Ah", we say, "This is good. All I need to do is borrow money to pay off my credit cards." A small voice urges us to ignore the added interest rates of the loan and payments to third parties who *help* us pay bills. The only thing they are helping us to do is to pay them more of our money, so they get richer.

Going into debt for the holidays has been an ingrained part of our lifestyles since childhood. Everyone does it. It's a normal way of life. It's been accepted by the masses, right or wrong. But now, positive attitude adjustment gives us a choice. We break away from the crowds, hold on to our life preserver, and stay debt-free, while still enjoying Christmas cheer.

Before PAA: Shoppers flitted helter-skelter through malls without a plan, buying here and there, without forethought. They were having a grand old time, adding purchases to credit cards.

There are many more self-destructive financial attitudes and actions that can be added to this list. Change our mindset. Using PAA, try the following ideas:

- Instead of every member of the family buying gifts for each other, have a drawing for each person.
- Purchase next years' decorations, cards, and anything else we need, immediately after Christmas for fantastic savings, if we have prudently left some money unspent.
- Keep a notebook handy throughout the year to jot down gift ideas for each person on our list. Watch for sales and purchase gifts ahead of time.
- Refrain from using credit cards for any gift unless the balance can be paid in full when the bill is due. Regardless of what others think, spend only the amount of money we can afford. There should be no exceptions.
- Purchase gifts conservatively. When buying expensive gifts with excess cash in our checking account, be aware of upcoming insurance premiums or other big payments coming due. Buying gifts on a lower plane brings security.
- Include gift purchases in the monthly income, not from credit cards, bonuses, or tax refunds.
- If there are current debts, do not compound the seriousness of the situation by purchasing more gifts.

We all want a merry holiday, but in some instances due to financial difficulties, we need to curtail spending. I am not advocating a Scrooge approach but it is no catastrophe for adults to forfeit gift giving until we are out of the bind. We can celebrate in other ways, like stocking gifts, a holiday outing or a dinner at home with reminiscing for dessert. Acquiring a new mindset is a joyous revelation.

Ahead of time, decide on a Christmas budget, not just for gifts. Include decorations, tree cost, entertainment costs, wrapping costs, hostess gifts, clothing, travel expenses, extra electricity charges, and any other costs we might have. Yes. This is a reality check. It's time to end rationalization and debt. Remember, we are the person it helps. We say, "But this takes all the fun out of the holidays." Stop. Think. Incurring debt during the holidays brings stress and worry. Spending within our means brings contentment and financial security. Isn't this more of a "fun" feeling?

How many of us can say we save twelve months out of the year? If we save only occasionally, skipping November, December, and January because of the holidays, blame only ourselves. Rationalizations make it harder to get back into savings mode. Rationalizations will continue to include summer vacations, Easter clothes, 4th of July celebrations, and before we know it, there are no savings deposits made at all. It all has been rationalized away and we now have credit card debt.

An alternative to replacing old decorations with new ones would be to make our own. "Yikes. Go back to the Dark Ages? No way!"

Remember the days of yore when Christmas decorations were made from gingerbread, ribbons, and popcorn? It could be great fun to go back in time and make our own. Have an enjoyable evening with family. Have a contest for the best original ideas. Serve hot apple cider and popcorn.

As a child, I made my own greeting cards and envelopes. Today we have a large variety of gift and card shops to choose from. Our imagination for making personalized cards has been replaced by the convenience of these stores. This should not force us to frequent them. Go back in time and have a blast. Design our own cards from personal thoughts and sayings for the special recipient.

Other ideas for saving money on greeting cards: Some discount stores have lovely cards for a fraction of the price of specialty stores, and computers can be used to create our own personal cards.

Gift boxes. We use the same ones year after year, throwing away only the unusable ones. We save boxes from every source, for size, stability, for gifts, for wrapping materials, mailing, and storage. We do not need to buy plastic storage containers.

Christmas storage boxes are used for lights, decorations, papers, etc. Before Christmas, get an idea of box sizes we will need for storing these items. Then, as we shop and see store employees restocking and discarding empty boxes; ask if we can take some. Don't wait too long. They usually flatten the boxes right there. Presto. Another freebee.

Many of us have hobbies and talents we can share with others. There's sewing, carpentry, repair skills, cooking, and a good strong back. A whole slew of knowledge is just waiting there to share with others during the holidays. Take advantage and save money.

Use our talents to make gifts instead of buying them. Baked goods, handmade sewing items, and carpentry items are examples. A handmade wooden shadow box is a perfect gift for someone that collects small figures. A scrolled window shelf valance makes a perfect way to display favorite knickknacks.

During the holidays, we get invited out to friend's homes. Instead of buying a gift for the host and hostess, make homemade bread, cake, or other baked items. If the friend has a favorite, we make that. A Christmas ornament is a good choice, as well as dollar stores and flea market items.

Live flowers are lovely gifts, but their life span is short. Instead of flowers, spend the same amount on something that can be enjoyed for many years.

Purchasing gifts for the elderly can present dilemmas. Are they bedridden, or in a wheelchair? The perfect gift is an oversized bib! Buy a large towel in their favorite color. Cut out a hole for the head and bind the rough edges. Sew on embellishments, ribbons, charms, etc. It covers them thoroughly and keeps their cloths clean. Take them a tape of their favorite music from their teen years. An aunt of mine, in a nursing home, cried tears of joyous memories as songs from the 1920s Charleston era wafted through the air. It was one of the best gifts she received in her later years. Any one of these gift ideas is easy on the budget. Neither gift was expensive, yet brought lasting use and enjoyment.

We can also offer assistance to the aged, by cleaning their home, changing light bulbs, taking them shopping, mowing lawns, or lifting and moving objects.

Put a limit on gift expenditures and stick with our decision.

Before PAA: We buy holiday logo shirts for Christmas, Easter, Halloween, Thanksgiving, and Valentine's Day. We wear them for a few days each year, and then store them until the following year.

After PAA: Instead of having special holiday clothes, we buy solid color shirts to wear all year and embellish them with holiday accessories, scarves, and jewelry. Then we are able to wear the clothes all year long, thereby, spending less money. We also buy household items in solid colors. For instance, a white tablecloth can be used for any occasion. For each holiday, use an appropriate centerpiece.

If Christmas savings accounts are passé in town, save at home. Each day, empty our pocket change into any container plus an extra dollar or two, and add money not spent on "it's only…." When November comes, count it out. That is our holiday money.

Scenario: Marcyann and Shakel have a good income, but barely make ends meet. They have friends whose incomes are similar but higher than theirs. They are pulled into a way of life of exchanging gifts for the holidays, anniversaries, and birthdays. The children exchange gifts, as well. These people don't hesitate to purchase expensive gifts, even if it means paying the rent or insurance premiums late.

PAA throws them a life preserver. Marcyann and Shakel sit down with their friends to discuss gifts and money issues. Instead of each family buying individual gifts, they all chip in for one nice gift per occasion. Cut back on occasions where gifts are bought. Keep Christmas and birthdays. Most likely everyone concerned will be relieved. Consider a delectable dessert party, a home cooked gourmet dinner, or a potluck dinner, instead of eating out.

Gifts for children: Our child wants five gifts for Christmas or a birthday. Have the child make a list of the gifts, making #1 the most wanted, #2 the next most wanted, and so on. It'll give the parents an excellent starting point, even if they can only afford several.

Scenario: Christmas and Birthdays. Hypothetically, children and grandchildren range in age from 4 to 12. There are about 20 gifts per child. Parents, family, and friends inundate the children with presents "because it's so cute" watching them unwrap the gifts. The repercussions are two-fold.

One. We are instilling wrong values. The child equates the more gifts received with more love and fun. They will form the idea it's a given. It's owed them now and in the future. There is nothing here that teaches inward appreciation. They will not be happy with less. Gone are reverence, holding things in esteem, and integrity. These attributes will not mean a hill of beans.

Two. Not only does the "give me, give me" mindset ruin a child's practical outlook on life, overspending also ruins the adult's financial stability. They both lose.

Buy practical toys that are made to last. Purchase gifts on sale. Pay bills as we go. If we have been teaching our children all along that money available to spend is what's left over after all bills have been paid, they will understand why gifts are given within a certain money range.

If children are interested in going on a school field trip or to a special vacation destination, buy gifts geared toward that. It's money well spent. Gift certificates are also wise present choices.

Before buying gifts to mail, perhaps sending a check instead will suffice. It not only gives the recipient the opportunity to get something they really want, but it also saves money on mailing postage and gift-wrapping.

Overall, purchase fewer and less expensive gifts.

If practical, start a toy trading and loaning library for the children in the neighborhood. Keep a log, name, and due date when toys or games need to be returned. The children now have many more options of things to do and play with. This is a huge money saver.

After adopting PAA think about how much money we spent on our children's gifts prior to learning we have choices. Then, spend 50% less on both gifts and clothing, then physically save and deposit the difference in a college account.

CHAPTER 12

BODY DRAPES

Before PAA, many of us, at one time or another, or continuously, purchased more clothes than we needed. This is called being a shopaholic. It's like a disease. Once it starts, it's almost impossible to curb it or to get cured from it. We get such highs going into stores, malls, discount stores, and specialty stores and coming home with shopping bags full of clothes and accessories. We don't give the shopping spree a second thought. We purchase clothes on sale because we save 20%, without realizing that we still have to pay the other 80%. We may shop because we're happy, sad, depressed, excited, or bored. We leave the house with our credit cards, debit cards, and checkbooks. We feel the excitement all the way to our destination, especially if there's a hot sale. What fun! We feel our adrenalin pumping. We can't wait to buy!

After exhausting ourselves from hours of shopping, and being heavily loaded down with bags, we trudge home with our bounty. Then, slowly, it hits us: the guilt and stress caused by our spending actions. If we were happy and excited before we went shopping, now the financial reality of it takes those feelings away, and sadness and fear replace it: fear of incoming bills, and sadness, knowing we are not able to pay for the all the purchases. This scenario is a prime example of self-sabotage.

After positive attitude adjustment, for the same reasons stated above, we go shopping. With us, is a list of clothes we *need*, not clothes we *want*. We shop at several places, compare prices, and sales. We go home with only the needed items. We have not overspent, and we feel good that we were able to get the best price. They'll not be any more purchases on our credit cards, because we planned for this shopping trip and paid cash. We still had fun.

We could plan a day of window-shopping. This is a good way to get out of the house. We leave our credit cards and checkbook at home. A minimal amount of pocket money will suffice. If we do find that special something, remember what store it's in. After going home and thinking about it, if it fits into our budget, and if it's a needed purchase, go back to the store several times, wait for a sale, then make the purchase.

Frequent trips to our favorite stores will familiarize us with the store inventory. For instance, new merchandise is on the front racks in the store for several weeks. Then it's gone for a few weeks, only to reappear on a sales rack.

Before buying new clothes, read the cleaning labels. The fewer "dry-clean only" clothes we purchase, the more money we save in dry-cleaning bills. Some "dry-clean only" garments can be safely washed at home with the proper detergents and cautions. Read labels on the detergent before using.

Do we need a new outfit for a special occasion? Be cautious. Try choosing a garment that doesn't require unique accessories. The special underwear, tie, shirt, shoes, and purse may double the purchase price.

If we are trying to impress someone by purchasing new expensive clothes, do not lose sight of the fact that it is us who must pay for it, not the one we are trying to impress. As long as we are neatly attired and clean, the rest of the scene will fall into place.

Judy's scenario: Thrift stores are great places to check out on a weekly or monthly basis. Some lucky person got a deal of a lifetime when I became allergic to wool. I donated four cashmere sweaters, a lined wool dress, and a pair of lined wool slacks. All were in new condition and all were purchased from Macy's. I also had donated many other clothes to a thrift store near my place of business. It was located in an upscale neighborhood, with mostly wealthy, retired people. At work, a short time later, in walked a "rich" customer wearing one of my donations! It goes to show you that shopping thriftily has no class boundaries.

We were going to a wedding, and John, who never wears a suit, needed a jacket. He found one, like new, with a designer label for $4.50 at the local thrift shop! And he received compliments.

When we moved north, I did not have any old jackets or jeans to use for outside work. At the thrift store I found a jacket for $3.50 and two pairs of jeans for $2.50 each. All these purchases were in good shape, as if the prior owner had grown into another size. Excellent clothing values can be found at flea markets, as well.

When shopping, we may find the perfect fit slacks. We can't make our mind up which color to buy, so we buy several in assorted colors. Before expanding the purchase this way, did we carefully think about how often we would wear them, if we have accessories to match, is the purchase within our budget, or will they just hang in the closet? Are we purchasing new slacks just for the thrill of it? Is our closet so full now that we would need to weed something out to make room for the new? No matter how great the new slacks are, do we really need them?

Is a special occasion on our horizon? Is it a tradition of the past that dictates buying new garments? Is it an ingrained automatic response? We have known from past experiences, that the special expenditure garment will be used maybe once or twice more before it ends up in the back of the closet. Before learning about PAA, we never once thought that there was another option. Now that we know better, we look in our closet, and see what will work this time, instead of buying something new. If anyone says,

"Hey, didn't you wear that last year?" Our reply might be "Considering the styles this year, this was by far the better choice." Or "I was so glad my outfit still fits that I could not help but wear it again."

Are we losing weight or gaining weight? Are we in a different size? Do we work in a large office where others are losing and gaining weight? Instead of buying a new wardrobe, exchange our clothes that don't fit with a fellow employee whose clothes will fit us. Presto! Not a penny spent! Have fun with it. Watch our other coworkers wonder what's going on.

There are times when clothes are important. However they need not be expensive. Professionals like to present themselves with a look equal to the task of their positions. This is fine. But to insure future financial stability, PAA suggests they would be wise to keep purchases within or below their earnings.

It is wise to begin a career thinking about our financial future. Avoid spending lavish amounts on career clothing immediately. Buy sensibly priced clothing until we are firmly established in our job. Remember, our life could change in a wink. Steer clear of going overboard and ending up in debt.

If we wish to cut back on clothing costs, there are several options. Buy from thrift stores, discount stores, and from regular stores conducting good sales. Buy cheaper. Buy fewer. When growing children are involved, swap used clothing with other families of growing children. The less spent on clothing for growing children, the more the family unit benefits. My son's feet grew four sizes in one school year. I saved money by buying him only one pair of shoes at a time, instead of buying several pairs and slippers.

Each lifestyle has its own way of disposing of expendable income, where to spend and where to save. What's feasible for one lifestyle may be detrimental to another. Each one of us needs to determine what's best for us. Remember that other people, TV commercials, and advertisements usually do not know what's best for any individual.

We need not accumulate shirts in every color to match all of the pants in our wardrobe. Stick to a few basic colors. When purchasing any type of clothing, basic colors are best: beige, navy, or black, with accessories in a few brighter colors. All basic colors can go with bright, dark or pastel colors. This same rule applies to other wardrobe accessories, as well; when a wardrobe consists of many colors, the cost of accessorizing them is an added expense.

The basic colors extend to makeup. I remember buying every color makeup and lipsticks. It wasn't cheap. No one cared if I had it all. I wore only one color at a time. A few basic colors would have sufficed. No one was ever fired for having too few colors in their makeup box! Perhaps we get a thrill out of buying the newest shades of cosmetics. But if we refrain from purchasing the extras, think of the thrill when we have saved the money instead.

A new fashion style appears. It's not a look that enhances our appearance, but it's a hot fad and everyone is buying it. Fortified with PAA, we are not tempted. We will wait until a more appropriate style comes out.

Sewing our own clothes is a money saver. I purchased my sewing machine and chair on sale. I buy fabric on sale and use coupons. I had sewing lessons from the store I bought the machine from. All of these things saved me money.

Recently, my bathrobe began deteriorating from old age. Thirty years ago, the robe cost $45. Replacing it today would be double that amount. The style was perfect. Robe styles today are different. I found fabric on sale, plus a 40% discount coupon. The total cost of the robe was $15. That's a $75 savings. I made the pattern for the new robe by ripping the pieces apart from the old robe and using them.

By learning to sew, men included, we will be able to make “originals”, mend our clothes, and make gifts. Remember to buy fabrics and notions on sale.

As we get self-assurance in the sewing arena, by all means, go into high fashion salons. We have a purpose, but not to buy. Look for fresh ideas on stylish outfits that we can duplicate on the sewing machine.

Have we ever purchased clothes that didn’t exactly fit right or weren't perfect for a special occasion? They end up in the back of the closet. In the meantime we still need that article of clothing. We go shopping again, carefully making sure of the fit this time. We buy this one, also. Whammy. Double expenditures.

If our weight fluctuates, buy inexpensive clothes on sale: just a few pieces in each size, to minimize money outlay. This is great for me. I have four sizes in the closet.

Costumes cost money. Instead of buying them, use old scraps of material, use our imagination, and make our own. If we need certain fabric, go to the thrift store and look through the merchandise. We could find the exact fabric we were looking for.

If we have purchased retail priced clothes recently, and they go on sale shortly thereafter, some stores will refund the difference within a specific time frame.

Outlet stores have fabulous prices for this year’s fashions. Try on the clothes before buying. It saves heartache later on: standing in long return lines, remembering the receipt, etc.

If we are not a high fashion person, purchase clothing at discount stores. They stay in fashion longer and we can wear them until they wear out. High fashion styles go in and out of style so quickly that replacements are needed sooner, costing us more money in the long run.

Clothing may acquire stains that won’t come out. I have a pair of pants with paint stains. The stores have oodles of new ones. I chose to wear the stained one for house and yard work. I didn't throw it out or buy a new pair. I saved money.

Does an undergarment have a small hole? Gees! We wear clothes on top of it. Why throw it out? There's still a lot of use in it.

Do we have a blanket, sheet, or a piece of clothing that has bleach stains? So what? The stain doesn't deem it unusable. Are sheets, towels, or clothing, old and threadbare? Keep them for rags or wrapping protectors for storage items.

Remember discount stores offer clothing at great bargains. For the price of one suit or outfit in a retail store, we could buy more than two in a discount store.

CHILDREN'S CLOTHING

Form a club of all parents from our child's school. Open a secondhand store for children's items. Parents should donate their children's clothes and toys that are still in good enough condition for another child to use them. Feel free to take sizes that fit our child. Purchasing scout uniforms this way are big money savers. Merchandise should be offered in a clean and pleasant atmosphere in order to attract parents from all walks of life. So, recycle is the key here. If there is no store available, have a parent donate space in their home or garage. Get a room in a pre-school, day school, or church. The location ideas are endless. The merchandise may even include musical instruments, sports equipment, school bags, and computer items.

As always, remember that you do not need to incorporate every suggestion in this chapter. Start slowly. PAA is accomplished step-by-step. Focus on the areas in our life that are currently draining our finances and begin to cut back in those departments. We will be glad that we did.

CHAPTER 13

HEALTH, MEDICAL, DENTAL, PRESCRIPTIONS AND VETERINARIANS

The first rule of economic freedom is to take care of our health. This rule and subtitles are financially interconnected to PAA and to our life preserver.

HEALTH and MEDICAL

Health and medical aspects of our lives go hand in hand to save money. The healthier we are, the fewer medical bills, and the more disposable income we save. So, why do some people jeer and laugh at others who follow healthy habits? Why are these people so afraid or defensive in responding to suggestions about healthier lifestyles? Maybe we need to cling to old ways as comfort mechanisms.

Another reason for disinterest in a healthier lifestyle is the assumption that anyone who engages in behavior not accepted as the norm must be a fanatic. Naturally, we wouldn't want to associate with these types of people. We are so afraid of change, that we don't want any part of it.

Stop! Think of the PAA life preserver. It benefits *us*! The people who are on a so-called health kick, if given the chance, can help us understand the benefits. Be open. Be inquisitive.

John had always eaten a healthy fare. So, while we dated he was eager to point out my unhealthy dietary habits. Awck! I wanted to scream, "Eek, let me out of here." Yes, his verbal attacks appalled me, but I knew he was right. It was apparent to me that John was healthy. He exercised daily, never had occasions to take medicines, and he had not seen a doctor in years. Thinking of the money he saved over time boggled my mind. As I transitioned to a healthier diet, his criticism ceased because he was delighted to see me taking better care of my health. He has contended, however, that his verbal attacks were not attacks, but his way of showing concern.

Just as I did not want John to be the only one in our family to have financial astuteness, I was not going to let him be the only one to have a healthy lifestyle. I saw tangible results. I gladly transitioned to better health, just as I had done with finances.

Before John taught me PAA, these are rationalizations I used in defense of my old, unhealthy eating habits. Parentheses are used to refute the rationalizations.

1. My eating habits do no harm. I feel great. (The intangible ill effects of unhealthy eating habits do harm our bodies. By not maintaining the highest quality of nourishment our cells, organs, and cardiovascular systems deteriorate, opening the door for disease.)
2. It's nobody's business. Stop heckling me to change. (It is other people's business. When we put our health in jeopardy, we put our family at risk. It is they who suffer the consequences when we get a disease. It's also everyone else's business that pays for health insurance. The healthier we are as a nation, the fewer medical bills, and the less we need to pay in insurance premiums.)

3. It tastes so good. I am not going to give it up. (There are many foods full of unhealthy fats, sugars, chemicals, and white carbohydrates that are delicious. There are other foods that are nutritious and just as delicious: fresh fruits and vegetables, nuts, lean meats, whole grains, fish, and poultry.)
4. I looked down in disgust at a friend's healthy foods. I chuckled under my breath and uttered, "Yuck. No one would catch me eating that stuff." (Now I am one of the health nuts myself because I know the benefits.)
5. Everyone dies from one thing or another. I want to enjoy myself. The heck with depriving myself of what I want to eat. (Witnessing friends and relatives suffering from avoidable illnesses from unhealthy eating habits was enough reason for me to change my diet.)
6. There's no proof that eating differently will make me healthier. (In fact, numerous magazine and newspaper articles, and television news reports quote the latest research findings, which confirm the benefits of healthful diets.)
7. It costs too much to buy health foods. (Yes, purchasing organically grown foods are more expensive than commercially grown foods. But we can alter our diets to include supermarket foods that have better ingredients such as whole grains, healthier choices of beverages, elimination of trans fats and

saturated fats, and elimination of sugars and high fructose.) PAA suggests raising an organic garden or bartering with someone who does.

These defensive statements are wake up calls alerting us to the way we rationalize our way to illness, disease, and death. It's black and white. There's no way to tread softly around this topic. Humans are made alike. We are susceptible.

When I changed my diet, it made me healthier and my body responded in a positive way: I had more energy, I was more alert, and I spent less on medicine because I hardly ever got sick. Occasionally, when I would sneak an old food from my past, my body would respond negatively. I'd feel sluggish. I couldn't concentrate as well, and I did not have the vital energy to hike or exercise as much.

Any tangible substance that goes into our body produces intangible effects that give it better health or slow destruction. Either we heed the warnings or suffer the consequences. Oral cancers, lung and throat cancers, diabetes, emphysema, heart and coronary diseases are not pretty pictures. They sap our strength, give us agonizing pain, and once we contract one of these diseases, it's usually too late to go back and change our lifestyle. The consequences of ignoring healthy lifestyles for years reach far and wide. Doctor, medication, and hospital bills can bankrupt us. Our family loses its ability to provide income, and our children can be psychologically scarred for life as they grieve over the loss of a parent.

We have a choice. We can change. We are responsible. Changing is easier when we surround ourselves with others that have the same views on health.

Our children not only are becoming diabetic, but they are also showing signs of coronary artery blockage and heart disease. This is devastating news for children and their parents, both emotionally and financially. We must reverse this trend. We must practice PAA in the health arena for the whole family.

John cannot stress enough how a healthy lifestyle saves astronomical amounts of anguish and money.

Scenario: Tiddalee is obese, eats an unhealthy fare, smokes, and does not exercise. He doesn't think of the health consequences this lifestyle will bring. He is completely oblivious to the damage he is causing his body. He has yet to learn of informative choices that can lead to a more beneficial way of life.

Let's look at what happens to him if he chooses to continue on his present destructive course. His body is like a machine that needs proper nourishing, maintenance, care, and activity. Without these things his body eventually breaks down and dies. And as his body deteriorates, his savings are used to pay medical bills. His life will be shortened and he will be cheated out of enjoying life and its wonders for many years.

Now look at Tiddalee since he's fortified with PAA and health related knowledge. He knows there are choices to make. He knows the consequences and attributes of his decision. He eats fish, lean meats, whole grains, and plenty of fruits and vegetables. He doesn't overindulge on sugar products. Nor does he smoke, use drugs, or drink alcoholic beverages. He exercises regularly and maintains a healthy weight. (Like John, he does not back down from his beliefs when offered something detrimental to his lifestyle and he still has fun, enjoys parties, and has an active life.) Tiddalee gets yearly physical exams as a defense against any unforeseen illness. As he grows older, like John, he maintains his stamina and good health, while around him he sees others his age with all sorts of physical maladies.

While these people go through traumas, financially, socially, and psychologically, Tiddalee continues to enjoy life. He increases the standard of his retirement with money saved on doctor bills.

So before we go poking fun at someone's health regime, like I did to my friend, let us think of the previous paragraph.

Exercise is an important part of our health regimen. Exercise is beneficial, and using the proper equipment is important. Machines include weight sets, treadmills, bikes, and rowing machines, to name a few. Before PAA, many new machines could have been purchased, and after awhile, they sat idle. After PAA we look at used machines. We find one for $450 that has 60 exercises. New, it cost $1,000. It includes all the exercises in our routine. Where do we find used machines? Look in the want ads in the newspaper or put an ad in the classified section, go on the Internet, and keep in touch with gyms in our area. They may be thinking of replacing some of their machines and would be happy to sell them to us for great savings.

Before starting an exercise program, ask our doctor if we are healthy enough to join a gym and if there are exercises we need to avoid. Visit several gyms, compare equipment; inquire about prices and discounts for paying quarterly and if they offer senior discounts. If we are joining a gym for the first time, ask if they provide a trainer to teach us proper workout techniques.

There are alternatives to working out at gyms and having our own home machines. We can walk up and down stairs, walk in malls during inclement weather and walk or hike outdoors, on the beach, to work, or to our favorite hangout. Swimming and dancing are exercise. These options cost less than gym dues or purchasing our own equipment.

John and I vary our exercise routine between our gyms, our home equipment that we use in bad weather, and outdoor activities, such as gardening, outside maintenance, walking, and hiking.

If our schedules are hectic and there's no time for exercise, try these alternatives: before lunch at the office, go for a short walk or do 10 minutes of isometric exercises, or if we are at home, clean house, do garden or yard work, or jog.

However, even the most conscientious efforts of living a healthy lifestyle cannot guarantee a disease free life. What they can give us is a better quality of life and a lower incidence of illness.

When we decide to change our health habits, it's an important step. At this time put PAA into high gear. The first change is always the hardest. Each subsequent one becomes easier. After a while we begin to feel better and have more stamina. When we do think of the old days and the unhealthy ways we treated our body, we will wonder how in the world we ever did it, for the appetite of the old ways has slowly diminished and disappeared.

Anything detrimental to our health, even though we feel good, should be cut way back or eliminated. This could be hard to do. Rationalization can rear its ugly head to center stage. It will try to disintegrate our attempt to change. Be aware. Do not let this happen. Have fortitude. Persevere through trial and error until the healthier lifestyle becomes habit. Our finances will sigh in relief as well as our body and mind.

The money saved on medical bills can pay for a lifelong dream vacation. This is one fantastic aspect of retirement: the time for us to do anything we choose. It's not a time to be an invalid with medical problems that could have been prevented.

My dad worked until he was 85. He maintained good health all through his life by avoiding fatty foods, sugared foods, and eating small portions of nutritious foods. He never smoked and took small sips of alcoholic beverages only to celebrate special occasions.

If we take care of our bodies throughout our lives, our bodies will take care of us in our senior years. Our good heath cannot be bought with dollars. It can only be obtained through consistent maintenance.

Staying healthy for a lifetime saves money on doctors, prescriptions, hospitals, loss of work, home care, etc.

There's an old saying that is so true: "You are what you eat." A woman who was a customer at my workplace, would come up to me, pointing and wriggling her long, skinny fingers in my face, like the wicked witch from Dorothy and the Wizard of Oz, saying just that. After a while, it sunk in. I changed to a healthier diet and I was sick far less. I built up my immune system and warded off viruses that ran rampant in my office. I actually felt better. I didn't catch a cold for four years. When I did catch a cold it was less severe and it did not automatically go into bronchitis. So for all of us who may think that woman was out of her mind, as I did at the time, think again. We are what we eat is a cliché, but it's true.

There are lifestyle diets and there are weight loss diets. Both incorporate PAA.

A lifestyle diet is a health conscious eating routine. By eating a certain way and drinking enough of the right types of liquids we enhance a prophylactic lifestyle. The foods and liquids ingested help our body to better health and fewer incidences of disease. This type of diet will entail some knowledge of healthy foods and beverages and require fortitude on our part. It consists of smaller portions, reduction or elimination of certain foods and additions of others.

I decided to further change some eating habits to incorporate foods that fight diseases that run in my family. They are diabetes, heart disease, coronary heart disease, and stroke. I didn't "go" on a diet. I cut quantity, eliminated high cholesterol foods, white carbohydrates, and sugar products. I ate more fruits and vegetables, lean protein, and whole grains. I weighed in about once a month and always saw weight loss. Weighing more frequently discouraged me. I lost thirty-five pounds in nine months and have leveled off with no weight gain for over six months. My entire system has responded in positive ways. If I just eliminate getting diabetes, I will save thousands of dollars in medication, not to mention worry about vision loss or the amputation of limbs.

Weight loss and fad diets are usually paid programs. They are a far cry from our healthy daily routine of eating. We either deprive our body of nutrients or we must eat only certain foods. We count points, we starve ourselves for X number of days, we eat only those foods that are not detrimental to our health, or we take diet pills. Weight loss diets are so numerous that it's hard to keep track of them. Why are there so many plans? It's because so few of them actually allow us to lose and keep the weight off. So why not get off the roller coaster of lose, gain, lose and gain? Try the lifestyle diet instead. It's cheaper and healthier. It doesn't cost a thing.

Some ideas to help get us get started on a healthier lifestyle:

1. Omit alcoholic intake or cut way back.
2. Eliminate tobacco in every form.
3. Don't even consider illicit drugs.
4. Eat less animal products. They contain cholesterol and saturated fats.
5. Eat more vegetables and fruits. The darker colored green vegetables have more nutritional value. For example, iceberg lettuce has less nutritional value than romaine or leaf lettuce. Green celery has more value than light yellow celery. Eat fruits in different colors to get a variety of vitamins and minerals.
6. Reduce sodium intake.

7. Replace white-floured products with whole grains. Processed white flour has little or no nutritional value. White carbohydrate foods include potatoes, rice, pastas, piecrusts, cakes, cookies and other baked desserts. (When I bake a pie, I make a flaky whole grain crust using olive oil.) It's as tasty as a piecrust made from white flour and saturated fat. For the recipe, go to: www.bobsredmill.com
8. Eat less harmful fats, which include hydrogenated, saturated, and trans fats. Good fats include flax, olive, canola, and omega 3 oils.
9. Maintain a healthy weight. It reduces chances for diseases and eliminates the expense of buying clothes in larger sizes. You feel better, too.
10. Drink soymilk instead of dairy milk. We drink soymilk flavored with vanilla. It tastes better and is healthier.
11. Wash hands often, especially after leaving the lavatory, and open the lavatory door with a tissue. There are people who don't wash their hands.
12. While out and about, get in the habit of keeping hands away from our face. Favorite entry places for germs are eyes, nose and mouth areas.
13. While in a doctor's office, always open doors with a tissue. Doorknobs are notorious for germ breeding.
14. Telephones and phone handsets are another place for germs. When using a phone other than our own, use caution

not to have the mouthpiece rub our mouth. If possible, wash our hands afterwards. When we respect and protect our health, it will take good care of us and allow us to save money by not getting sick.

The great American marketing machine knows we are planted in front of the television. While we relax in our immobile lifestyle, we are subjecting ourselves to obesity, diabetes, and heart and arterial diseases. They know they have our undivided attention to sell us unhealthy goods, which further promote bad health. If we want to slouch in front of the television set, why not exercise at the same time? Lightweight barbells, abdominal stretches, and other exertions are healthy ways to keep our bodies in shape.

The great American marketing machine's propaganda has succeeded in programming society into accepting advertised foods and medicines as good for us, without checking the reliability of the health aspects. In the past we assumed anything advertised was good for us. Now we know differently. Genetically engineered foods and new medicines have not been tested long enough to know long-range health implications. Consumers need to question the reliability and truthfulness of food and medicine ads and then do what is in their best interest.

Choosing a new doctor is an important decision. Ask family, friends, coworkers, or gym buddies for referrals. Find out if our new doctor has had malpractice lawsuits or peer reviews and the outcomes of those cases. A peer review is an alternative to lawsuits, where in a dispute, doctors (or dentists) are tried by their peers. This is free. A lawsuit costs money. For medical, call The American Medical Association, 1-800-621-8335. For dental, call The American Dental Association, 1-800-621-8099.

Find out if a certain doctor is part of our insurance group.

Ask if there is a charge for calling the office for information, making an appointment or canceling one, or refilling a prescription. If a doctor tells us that all doctors charge for these things, look for another doctor. This happened to me when we moved to Montana. I called other doctors and found out they don't all charge. In fact, very few did. I changed doctors.

Ask what rules apply when there's a nurse practitioner available, and if the office visit is cheaper. Will the practitioner call in the doctor when the scope of our problem calls for higher skills? Or will the nurse make a vain attempt to make a diagnosis? Always ask to see the doctor if we feel uneasy.

Perhaps there are several things we would like to discuss with the doctor, but none are urgent. Keep a list. Then when we see the doctor, we will be paying for one office visit, while getting multiple questions answered.

Ask the doctor for information on immune system enhancers. They build up our resistance to sickness, thereby reducing doctor and prescription bills.

The doctor should be on the same wavelength as we are. Some doctors don't take the time to really listen and as a result, they may advise us badly or do things detrimental in our particular case. The end result could cost us more money and heartache, or even an allergic reaction.

If we are on an HMO, ask the doctor whether he will refer us to a specialist, as needed. While I was on an HMO, my primary physician would not send me to a specialist when my right arm was stuck. (He said he only sends important cases to specialists.) When my husband heard that, he flew into a rage! Finally, after threatening the doctor, I was allowed to see a neurosurgeon. Yes, I had a spur on my cervical spine. He thought it was the cause of my stuck arm. Without further tests, he performed surgery to remove the spur. Surprise! After the surgery, my arm kept getting worse. My primary doctor was a little nervous, as was the neurosurgeon when they realized I had been misdiagnosed.

I was sent to a neurologist. Within five minutes, he diagnosed my problem as a frozen shoulder. This medical breach cost my HMO over $14,000, and $2000 out of our pocket, for an unnecessary surgery and a long painful recuperation for me. Moral of my story: If we need a specialist and we are on an HMO, insist on a second opinion before any surgery and do not stint on asking for further tests. It will save us money.

If we have positive lab test results, insist on having new lab tests and sending them to another lab for testing. Many mistakes occur in labs!

Some doctors give free skin cancer screenings. Take advantage of the offer.

Hospital bills add up, even after insurance payments. Some hospitals charge interest on unpaid balances. We made a deal with our hospital while I was on an HMO, after two simultaneous stays, one for a broken leg and one after a blood clot. If the bills of $4,000 (two insurance deductibles of $2,000) were paid in full within four months, there would be no interest charged. We cut back to the bone. If we had any outstanding credit card bills to pay, we could not have paid the hospital in four months. Paying off the bill was next to impossible, but we managed. We didn't touch savings.

John never smoked or used alcoholic beverages. He has not only preserved his health, which saved money, but these are the amounts he saved by not partaking in smoking and alcohol:

Smoking: 1 pack a day at $4.79 a pack for a year:	$1,748.3
Cost over 10 years:	$17,483.50
Cost over 40 years:	$69,934.00
Alcoholic beverages: Bar tab for 1 year:	$1,000

Cost over 10 years:	$10,000
Cost over 40 years:	$40,000
Total costs not spent:	$109,934.00

It is impossible to estimate further savings from not having medical or prescription expenditures.

PRESCRIPTIONS

Medications can be costly, but there are a number of ways to conserve money, and obtain high quality treatment.

Use these guidelines when we need prescriptions:

1. Ask for samples.
2. Ask for the least expensive medication, which has the same benefits as the more expensive ones.
3. Ask for generics.
4. But the most important thing is that the FDA has approved the use, by the public, of many new prescription drugs that have not undergone long-term testing. Many people die every year from complications and side effects from taking some of these new drugs. When my doctor wants to prescribe a new medicine, I insist that he prescribe an older, time-tested drug, to insure its safety. Doctors prescribe prescriptions that are pushed by pharmaceutical company salespersons, so I call this the great American prescription sales con. We, the consumers, must become aware of this phenomenon to protect ourselves against this potentially deadly practice. Medications that have been on the

market for a number of years are cheaper than newer ones and have generics, which also cost less.

Get to know our pharmacist. My pharmacist constantly looks for money savers and makes suggestions to improve my knowledge and use of medications.

When a prescription calls for 250mg twice a day, ask for the 500mg and cut them in half. If it calls for 10mg, ask for 20mg and so on. We would be surprised at the savings.

There are medications that we take over a long period of time. Sometimes, if we work hard on changing the causes for that illness, we can wean ourselves off the medication, saving big bucks. Talk to our doctor first. Put everything in perspective. For instance, a high cholesterol pill costs $100 a month, or $1200 a year. Our doctor can advise us of things to do that reduce cholesterol count. Some things are to exercise, reduce saturated fats and high cholesterol foods, and lose weight. This entails some work. So? Is the value of the work commensurate with the money saved and better health? If we saved this kind of money in other areas, as well, just imagine what kind of savings we would have accumulated in a year!

Author's scenario: When I changed my diet regimen to avoid diseases that ran in my family, my cholesterol dropped from over 200 to 137. I went off the cholesterol prescription and saved $100 a month.

Do we have a new or refillable prescription that needs to be filled? We don't owe allegiance to any one pharmacy. Call every pharmacy in our area for price quotes. Then, buy the cheapest. If we prefer doing business with just one pharmacy, ask them to meet the cheaper price. Tell them we would like to continue doing business with them, but it's up to them to meet the price. Sometimes they do so in order to retain our business. If they can't meet the price, go where it's cheaper and don't feel guilty. I was going to a particular pharmacy that gave senior discounts. I found another pharmacy with cheaper prices.

Some pharmacies advertise they will meet competition prices. Others, we have to ask.

Mail order pharmacies can be cheaper still, but check out their reliability. They have less overhead expenses than retail drug stores. But, always compare prices. Do not take anything for granted.

If we take medication on an ongoing basis, bottles of 90 or 100 are cheaper than buying 30 at a time. Sometimes a simple aspirin works as well as an expensive prescription medication. Case in point: For back pain I use to take Lodene 500mg at a cost of $44 for 30. I tried an Aleve (a bottle of 50 cost $4.97) and it works just as well. John's doctor prescribed Celebrex 200mg for his arthritis at a cost of $98.99 for 30. Instead of filling the prescription he tried Aleve and it took the pain away.

Living in close proximity to Canada or Mexico also gives us a financial edge to save money on prescriptions. John and I have never been disappointed with the quality of medications from either Canada or Mexico.

Some of the advertised propaganda says Canadian medications are inferior to their US counterparts. Every medication we buy in Canada has been manufactured in the US. They are not inferior. Think of it this way: Would Canada manufacture substandard medications for their citizens? Of course not! We would love to be able to have allegiance to the US, but they make it impossible, price-wise.

We have also gotten prescriptions filled in Mexico. For instance, Cipro, an antibiotic, cost us $78 for 20 pills in Yuma, AZ. When we refilled it in Mexico, we got 36 pills for under $20 US. The pills were manufactured in the US.

So, before buying prescriptions, compare prices. Use the suggestions here to help in the search.

Prescription drugs, vitamins, over-the-counter medicines, and supplements have expiration dates, which tell us how long they will retain potency, and are printed on the containers by the pharmaceutical companies that manufacture them. However, many of these medicines' potencies stay strong beyond the printed expiration date. Our doctors are our best source of information to find out which ones retain potency beyond the date listed.

Proper care of prescription medications, vitamins, supplements, and over-the-counter drugs protect their potency and extend their life. Freezing temperatures, excessive heat, bright light, and humidity deteriorate medicines. Keep them in a cool, dry place, away from direct sun and do not leave them in a parked car where temperatures climb.

When we take care of our health, eat nutritionally, and exercise, we have less chance of getting sick and needing prescriptions. Changing our mindsets and being aware of these actions save us money.

DENTAL

Smoking and diet play a financial role here, as well. Tobacco products stain teeth and contribute to gum recession and disease, and oral and other cancers. Visit an oral cancer ward in a hospital to see firsthand the horrors and agonies.

Having gum recession, a periodontal disease, could lead to expensive dental work or even dentures. Vow to work hard on our own oral hygiene. It will save us money in the long run.

Some foods are harmful to teeth. Sugar foods top the list for starting cavities and decay. Sugar means candy, cookies, pies, cakes and other desserts, snack foods, sodas, chewing gum, fruits and fruit juices, and a slew of other foods. After eating citrus fruits, which are high in acid, and after ingesting sugary foods, it's wise to rinse our mouth out with water.

Parents need to ask the pediatrician when to start dental hygiene for their children. Then, pediatric dentists can teach children proper brushing techniques. As the child learns to brush, the parents should supervise, making sure that it is being done correctly. Not having the proper brushing techniques can lead to tooth decay and dental bills. While children are learning, do have a positive, relaxed attitude, not a dictatorial one. They'll respond likewise with a positive attitude. Dentists recommend teeth should be cleaned twice a year. When children are old enough, have the hygienist show them proper flossing. Again, this is a money saver. Filling cavities is not cheap.

My childhood dental hygienist had a plaque on the wall, which read, "Floss Only the Teeth You Wish to Keep." The reward of flossing correctly is that our mouth remains healthy, therefore, we require less dental work, and that allows us to save money.

Everyone's mouth is a little different. Some of us have to do more than just brush and floss, while many others do not. Our dentist can show us the best hygiene for our mouth.

Good dental hygiene has its benefits. As a rule, the cleaner our teeth and mouth are, the fewer and smaller the cavities. Larger fillings may lead to cracked and broken teeth, leading the way to expensive crown and root canal work, or even dentures.

A disadvantage to caring for our teeth and health is that the benefits cannot be seen with our eyes. People react more to tangible things. With health and teeth, there are no tangibles. By eating correctly, we don't *see* how our bodies respond. Likewise with poor dental hygiene, we can't *see* our cavities being born or our gums starting to recede. By making ourselves aware of these pitfalls, we can act accordingly in keeping our bodies and teeth healthy.

Neither do we *see* our bodies acting favorably to exercise. All these intangibles are at the core of a healthy body and mouth.

Most of us are aware that if we are faced with a large medical procedure, we seek a second opinion. I strongly advocate we start doing the same thing for dental procedures, as well.

Judy's scenario: I was told I needed seven crowns and a root canal, costing close to $8,000. The crowns were for teeth filled with amalgam, which over the years expanded, thus causing cracks in some teeth. The root canal was for another tooth that had a deep filling and was causing pain. I sought another opinion. I didn't need any crowns. I needed one onlay that covers one quarter of the tooth and costs far less than a crown. The second dentist removed all the amalgam fillings, replacing them with composite material that seeps into the cracked parts of the teeth and acts as a form of glue. As far as the root canal was concerned, the second dentist suggested waiting a while to see if the nerve would repair itself. It did. We saved $6,000.

VETERINARIANS

Do we have a favorite veterinarian that we have taken our pets to for a long time?
Have we ever once thought of comparing their rates with other veterinarian rates?

My daughter had been taking her six cats to the same veterinarian for years until she decided to call other veterinarians to compare prices. She found that hers was the most expensive in her area. She changed and saved over 40%!

When deciding on a new veterinarian, discuss shots, yearly checkups, prices, discounts, new technologies and treatments, the cheapest and most expensive medications, office hours, times to make appointments, and how to save money wherever possible.

Keep pets healthy. Exercise them daily, prevent them from overeating, getting fleas, and check their teeth because plaque buildup can cause decay and the infection can spread to the bloodstream.

Good Housekeeping gives these veterinarian money saving tips:

1. Seek a second opinion before having a surgical procedure.
2. Buy pet food and supplies in bulk, through pet discounters, such as Petland and Petco. Buying from vets or grocery stores cost more money.
3. Keep careful medical records, just as we would for ourselves. This way, vets will not give unnecessary shots to your pet, and you do not pay for repeated treatments.
4. Ask about vaccines and if it is cheaper to get them once every three years instead of every year.
5. Try pet clinics. Go to www.pets911.com for a list of local clinics.
6. Ask for multiple-pet rates

CHAPTER 14

FINANCIAL STABILITY KILLERS TOBACCO, ILLICIT DRUGS, ALCOHOL, AND GAMBLING

This chapter will probably incur some wrath. I have no power or inclination to tell us to stop using these products. I will show the serious consequences and how widely spread they are and how, by purchasing them, we disintegrate our long-term financial goals.

SMOKING AND TOBACCO RELATED PRODUCTS

Many of us succumb to smoking because of peer pressures, family/social/personal problems, and/or our desires to emulate parents, friends, media, or people in the entertainment industry.

Children may begin smoking at such an early age that parents have not had time to discus its dangers or how they can just say "no." I suggest, from my own experience, parents should discus the ravages of tobacco related products in everyday conversations within hearing distance of their young children. As with indoctrinating children with PAA at an early age, the same holds true with tobacco abstinence.

Once we begin using tobacco and related products, it becomes addictive. When we buy our chosen "cancer death wish weed", in essence, we are tossing our hard earned money into a bonfire of hell. We are willingly handing our money over to the large tobacco corporations. They say "Thank you" while we are making them wealthy, and they, in turn, are slowly depleting our finances and destroying our health. "Hey," we say. "We are feeling fine." Sure we are. We think we are immune to the side effects. They only happen to others. Surprise! Go to any hospital. Speak to cancer patients whose voice boxes have been removed. Speak to those who contracted emphysema, oral cancer, coronary disease, lung cancers and heart attacks, all from smoking. Every one of those people said the same thing. "I feel fine. It'll never happen to me." It seems that some people seem to escape the ravages of tobacco related illnesses for years…until…finally a disease hits. Then, it's too late. An old cliché says it all, "An ounce of prevention is worth a pound of cure."

It's incomprehensible to knowingly spend money on poisonous weeds that we put in our mouth, catch them on fire and inhale that poison while destroying our health.

When we do contract a tobacco related disease, our entire family is affected, as well as friends and coworkers. We will leave our mate alone, our children will be forever scarred by a loss of a parent, and our friends will mourn the loss of enrichment we brought into their lives. Our loss, due to an avoidable addiction, deprives all these people forever of our presence.

The pros for smoking are none.

The cons are numerous:

1. Constriction of arteries causing shortness of breath, reduced stamina, strength, and ability to concentrate.
2. Leads the way to heart, lung, respiratory diseases, strokes, cancers, and emphysema.
3. Since tobacco is an addiction it's extremely difficult to give up.
4. Our entire family suffers. From secondhand smoke, we in turn are subjected to the same smoker's

illnesses. Even pets die from emphysema and cancer caused by our smoking.

5. Tobacco related illnesses put the entire family into financial crisis.
6. Hypothetically, the family breadwinner contracts emphysema and heart disease from smoking. He's unable to work and his children's college funds are quickly eaten up by excessive medical needs. All this could have been easily avoided by saying a simple "no" when a first cigarette was offered to him.
7. Think back through all the years of smoking. Add up all the money spent, be it for cigarettes, cigars, pipes, chewing tobacco, lighters, or what not. Include costs of replacing clothing, furniture, or rugs that had tobacco burns. Don't rationalize. Add everything. Would it have been enough for a whole life insurance policy, paying off a mortgage, going to Tahiti, or financing retirement? And all this money, not there, due to a preventable habit. How sad.
8. A parent dies from smoking related illness and is not around to enjoy the blessings of seeing his children and grandchildren's continued life's cycle.
9. How would we like to have a cancerous voice box removed and speak through a hole in our neck for the rest of our life, only to find that in a year's time, the cancer spread to our lungs? So I plead, weigh the pros and cons using PAA and

reality. Reach for the life jacket. Save us, save our family, and save our finances from the horrors of tobacco. For those who choose not to quit, be aware that the human body is the same for everyone. Ours is not immune.

10. There can be no rationalization or sympathy here. We have only one body and once it's abused, that's it. There's little or no chance of reversing the damage. There's no wishful thinking "if only." We did it. We had a choice. Now we pay the consequences.

If we are a smoker and realize it's damaging our body and we would love to be able to stop, there are several avenues open. Ask our doctor what is available and what is recommended.

National Smoker's Quit Line offers an array of help for smokers who wish to quit. Their phone number is 1-800-784-8669. Nicotine Anonymous also offers choices and programs. They can be reached at http://www.nicotine-anonymous.org/ or phone them at 1-631-665-0527.

The best advice I can give smokers who seriously want to quit is to read *Stop Smoking for Good,* by Balasa L. Prasad, MD. He has an unprecedented approach, one that works permanently without the aid of chemical quitting agents.

The money saved, as we rid ourselves from tobacco addiction, should be used to make dreams come true and reach financial goals.

We will be glad we quit, not only because of the health risks, but also because tobacco smells; it stinks, and it makes us stink as well.

ALCOHOL

Uh-oh, here comes another one. "Oh, no, I just have to have a drink. I love it. It goes with smoking. It goes with TV sports programs. It goes socially; alcohol tastes so good. What are ya doin'? Ya want to deprive me of all my enjoyments!"

I say to you, "Read this chapter again after rereading the PAA chapter".

Okay. I'll begin listing the attributes of alcohol first, to soothe our mind.

There are none. This is a reality!

The detrimental effects could be one or more of the following, usually many more than one.

1. Deterioration of the liver
2. Alcoholism and alcohol poisoning
3. Mood swings: Jekyll and Hyde personality traits emerge
4. Embarrassment
5. Violence
6. Endangering lives of others and our own
7. Breakup of the family unit
8. Unable to focus clearly when decisions need to be made
9. Memory brain cells permanently damaged
10. Being sued for everything we have due to injuring or causing death to another person while intoxicated
11. Unable to perform job duties.
12. Crippling children for life, leaving some children orphans, or taking away a family's income while one spouse cares

for an injured bedridden loved one, due to an accident caused by intoxication.

13. Can we think of more detrimental reasons?

As in other situations cited in this book, add up all the costs for our alcohol use for one year. Don't fudge. Add up bar tabs, beers for viewing sports events on TV, purchased alcohol for our home, and gifts. Is the dollar amount enough to have eliminated all those times we have said, "But I just never seem to have enough money?"

Call or look on the Internet to contact any Alcoholics Anonymous Services.

SUBSTANCE ABUSE AND MINORS

Let us include our children as we change our mindsets to permanently live debt-free.

Children who grow up witnessing their parents using tobacco products, alcoholic beverages, illicit drugs, and know that they gamble, are at risk for partaking in these destructive activities, as well. Parents should be role models. Most parents automatically teach their children how to safely cross streets, never talk to strangers, and never to try drugs. But how many parents teach their children the detrimental effects of tobacco, alcohol, and gambling? These desperately need to be added to this list. The money paid for these destructive substances eats up money more wisely spent for college educations.

Some guidelines for parents who want ideas on how to protect their children from the dangers of all financial security killers:

1. Have open communications with our children where many subjects are discussed, including smoking, drinking alcohol, taking illicit drugs, and gambling. Draw out their innermost

feelings and thoughts concerning these topics. Compare our present lifestyle with one ravaged by the detrimental consequences of using these substances and gambling.

2. Discuss peer pressure as opposed to standing up for what the child knows is right. Play act a scenario of what the child can do and say if presented with a chance to try smoking, alcohol, drugs, or gambling.
3. Know the families of our children's friends. Discuss their ideas and thoughts on tobacco use, alcohol and drugs, and gambling. Make sure their views are in line with ours because there are some parents that see nothing wrong with allowing their children to engage in these activities.
4. Chaperone ALL children's parties, while they do homework with friends, and where children are gathered.

ILLICIT DRUGS

There is not one good reason to partake in the use of illicit drugs. Every rationalization is dangerous to our health, our future, and to all our family members and our friends.

If we are using drugs presently for enjoyment, think again. Even though we may not be aware of the drug's intangible destructiveness within our body, over a period of time, those drugs are surely enjoying worming their venom on our body. The drugs are laughing in glee over their mission of ruination because they know we have absolutely no idea what's going on.

What are the financial pitfalls of taking drugs? Some people are so desperate for their drug fix that they rob their families, friends, and strangers for the money needed to support their habit. If we are a drug user, try adding up the total amount of money that we have thrown away on drugs, if that is even possible. Some people's minds may be unable to calculate how much money they have wasted. If they could add up what they have already spent, along with the amount of money that they may spend on drugs in the future, they would be aghast. Did they ruin their chance of having a college education, money for a new career, and an opportunity to have a loving family?

Do we need a high? Don't reach for drugs or alcohol. Go for a jog, go for a walk and enjoy the beauty of Mother Nature or start an exercise routine instead.

There is help for those addicted to drugs. Talk to school counselors, deans, doctors, or religious leaders to be put in touch with rehabilitation centers. Any of these sources can direct us toward helping put our lives back on track.

Fortified with PAA, and knowing the effects from drug usage, those of us who do not use, will have the willpower to say NO, in any situation. By not throwing out money to purchase illicit drugs, we are able to reach our financial goals and have a productive life.

GAMBLING

Gambling is another activity that can drain savings and put us in debt.

The Montana Council on Problem Gambling, a non-profit agency, is dedicated to alleviating gambling-related social and personal distress through the provision of relevant support, referral services, and education to compulsive gamblers, their families and other concerned Montanans (our state here).

According to the Montana Council on Problem Gambling, approximately 6-9 million Americans are estimated to have difficulty with gambling at a cost of $5 billion per year. Imagine what this amount of money could do to improve personal financial stability; it could even provide higher levels of education and medical insurance for all Americans.

What causes people to gamble too much? Susan Edgar, program director for the Delaware Council on Gambling Problems, says the reasons are multifaceted. Initially, it is fun and feels good, and it is a way of socializing with others. Some people progress from the pleasurable aspect into being habitual gamblers. What starts out as a penny-ante entertainment could escalate into compulsive gambling and create a nightmare of enormous financial losses. To have fun and keep our finances secure, we would do better to choose activities that do not include gambling.

Casinos purposefully provide an environment of excitement that includes loud music, psychedelic lighting, and sounds of dancing coins. We revel in this pseudo-induced euphoria. The more we feel our adrenaline exploding, the more confident we become that we can beat the system. However, at the end of our casino visit we not only leave, we leave our losses there, as well. Habitual gamblers have colossal losses, much more than just money. Families are torn apart, homes and jobs are lost, and lives are lost due to suicide.

For some of us, we can handle an occasional gambling outing, only spending a certain amount, say $20, and when that's lost, we stop. This is good and bad. It's good because we have the willpower to stop. It's bad because when we gamble $20 a week for entertainment, times 52 weeks a year, times that for 10 years, we have spent $10,400 of our hard earned money. Did we stop to realize, before we gambled, that it was another “it’s only” purchase?

Author’s scenario: While I worked at the bank in Hollywood, Florida, the employees got together once a year to fly on a junket to the Bahama Islands for 12 hours of gambling. Once I joined my colleagues. I watched them as they turned into excited, robotized creatures being pulled like magnets to the gambling frenzy. They scurried around not quite knowing which machines or tables to try their luck. I witnessed, firsthand how those psychedelic lights, loud music, and sounds of dancing coins transfixed normal intelligent people into gambling away their hard-earned money, all in the name of fun.

I tried my luck at the slot machines with my measly $5.00 in change. This was the first and last time I gambled. Within five minutes I lost all of it. Fun? Each time I pulled down the lever I had a sinking sensation in my chest. I knew I was out of my league. This gambling was not for me. I spent the remainder of the long night observing the other employees losing their money, as well.

The occasional gambling outing can grow into a habitual addiction, and either one can destroy financial security. If gambling starts to overrun our lives, there is help. The National Council on Problem Gambling can assist. The phone number is 1-800-522-4700.

There is also a concept called self-exclusion, which many casinos offer. This program is for gamblers that want to quit, but find it hard to do. Gamblers go voluntarily, through casino managers, owners, and/or security personnel, to fill out the self-exclusion form which includes a photo ID of the gambler. If the gambler is seen in the casino after the form has been filed, there are consequences such as fines or being arrested. Keith Whyte of the National Council on Problem Gambling tells me self-exclusion varies from jurisdiction to jurisdiction, and sometimes even within the area, depending on what type of gambling is available. So if gamblers do not want entrance to several different gambling establishments, they need to sign these forms in each location.

Donna Johnson, executive director of Montana Council on Problem Gambling recently gave my number to Rick Rice. He told me that after years of a gambling addiction, his beloved wife took her own life. Their story was so poignant and heartbreaking, we both cried as he related both catastrophic emotional and financial losses. He wishes to spend the rest of his life putting together programs to help others ovoid his anguish and help stem the tide of problem gambling.

An excellent book to help gamblers conquer their addiction is *Stop Gambling for Good*, by Balasa L. Prasad, MD with Catherine Whitney.

Conclusion: We need to eliminate all these financial security killers that prevent us from reaching our financial goals.

Do not be pressured by peers to drink, smoke, take illicit drugs, or to gamble.

Do not turn to financial security killers to relieve stress or problems. Instead, seek the beauty of Mother Nature, favorite hobbies, exercise, or professional help. And, remember, there is no stigma attached to just saying "No" when we are first offered any of the financial security killers.

I advocate that the heads of each organization of financial security killers begin a progressive plan of attack to research why people try their first tobacco product, first alcoholic beverage, their first illicit drug, and their first gamble. Then hone in on the reasons and offer an advanced educational plan for schools, parents, and professionals that will prevent these firsts.

CHAPTER 15

HOBBIES

Hobbies are activities or interests pursued for pleasure or relaxation. They bring contentment into our lives or fill us with exhilaration.

Some hobbies come out with newer additions, technologies and updates.

When we go overboard financially with such an enjoyable outlet, we defeat our purpose of reigning in our spending. When the credit card bills come in with enormous charges, our hobby turns into a nightmare of debt and stress. It's comparable to a sickness or addiction. Once we start supporting our hobby with credit card purchases, the more we do it. Soon we have multiple credit cards, all charged to the limit.

Beware of these pitfalls. Power to avoid them first comes with knowledge and understanding of the situation before it occurs.

When we react in a certain way long enough, it becomes ingrained. We know of no other way. But when an alternative solution is presented, it's the first time we realize there's another choice available. Embrace it. Act on it. Use our life preserver, PAA, as a guide to change our mindsets so as to curb hobby expenditures.

Are we a jigsaw puzzle enthusiast? Buy them at garage sales or secondhand stores. Most cost twenty-five cents to a dollar. Or start a puzzle club with others who enjoy puzzles. Check puzzles out like a library card, from club members.

Scenario: Little tiny stuffed animals in all shapes, forms, and colors, were the fad of the day. Without thinking of financial repercussions, we ran out and purchased all the latest ones to add to our collection. We surrounded ourselves with these *things.* They made us feel warm and happy. Several years later, when the little animals were not the rage anymore, and were stored away in the attic, we wondered why we spent so much money on them. This was especially apparent when, unexpectedly, we needed a new transmission for our vehicle. We realized the money spent on our stuffed animal hobby would have been more wisely spent (saved) to cover the unexpected contingency of the new transmission. This same story can be played out in a myriad of other scenarios.

When we moved north, we purchased all of our ski and exercise equipment at garage sales and secondhand stores. This saves big bucks.

If we are music enthusiasts, borrow and lend within our circle of music friends. Tape what we want and return the original in a timely manner.

In the past we might have had everything we wanted for our hobbies, including systems and the newest in technology. We charged it all, even items that were on sale. What good is the money saved on a sale if we pay out the savings in interest payments? These eye openers are for any hobby.

Does our child have a hobby that includes a doll or a military figure? Does each one come with a zillion accessories? Does our child want every one? Let him show us which ones he really wants. That’s it. No more. Stand our ground.

As we suggest these money savings techniques with friends, they should give us a positive reaction since it will open up new money savings’ ideas for them, as well.

No matter what our hobbies are, these suggestions can fit into them. Add other ways we can save money on our hobbies to this list.

CHAPTER 16

IN THE WORKPLACE

This is a perfect place to examine positive attitude adjustment in a different arena other than for finances. Let's change our mindset from the status quo and wear our life preservers to work.. Prioritize PAA into our working environment to improve the atmosphere. Identify problem areas, eliminate negativism and self-entitlements, and have dedication and motivation to change. As we make constructive changes, fewer old problems remain. Have fortitude to go the extra mile, take courses to enhance our work knowledge, and volunteer for extra projects. All these things increase job performance and may lead to pay raises.

Now let's see where we can save money on the job. We can start by car pooling, walking, bicycling, or taking a bus or subway to get to and from work instead of driving our vehicle.

Avoid toll roads unless it's absolutely the only way to arrive at our place of business.

Working spouses or significant others: Is the money earned more than the expenditures that are required for the job? Figure in wardrobe, an extra vehicle, insurance and maintenance, gas, paying for childcare, and incidentals.

Do vendors pop into our office to sell things such as jewelry, books, utensils, handcrafted items or cosmetics? Before buying on impulse, ask ourselves if we were looking for the item anyway, and if it will it be within our budget. Most times we wouldn't be able to justify the expense.

Purchase a career wardrobe and accessories at discount stores or sew our own. Take advantage of department store sales. After all, we are working to support ourselves and to save money, not to flaunt expensive cloths and go into debt. Remember I worked a second job at Macy's and ended up paying them more than I made because I used their credit card for employee discounts. Boy. Did I learn a lesson!

Buy multiple piece outfits. Mix and match. Don't feel we need different clothes for every day of the month. Avoid dry-clean only garments unless we dry-clean them ourselves.

Is a coworker's birthday coming up? Is there a collection being taken to purchase a gift? Was there an employee meeting held and an agreement reached on each employee's share of the cost? Could everyone agree on a given amount? Maybe someone in the office had a recent vehicle repair, or other large expenditure and extra monies are not available. Or maybe someone is barely making ends meet. Make sure the collections don't put anyone in financial jeopardy. It could be embarrassing and awkward.

Do not go along with coworkers when they are spending money for an office gift just because it's come to be expected. If we cannot contribute the amount requested, suggest a less expensive alternative or diplomatically bow out. Stand our ground! We should never spend money on something just because others are doing it. They don't pay our bills. We do.

Many offices have lunches delivered. Figure out if the expenditure easily fits into our budget. If we order once a week and spend $6.00 that is $312 a year, which is enough to pay our prescription drug bills. To refuse, try using one of these reasons: "Sorry, not today, no thanks, some other time, I've already browned bagged it today, I'm on a special diet, or I'm having stomach problems." Even if everyone else orders out, stand our ground. We are saving money. Do not be tempted. One more thought here: we could order out for a very special occasion.

I always brought my own lunches to work. If I had bought lunch for $5.00 a day, five days a week, for a year, the cost would have been $1,300! Over 20 years I would have spent $26,000! But I chose to buy lunch ingredients at the supermarket for $20 a month or $240 a year, or $4,800 over 20 years, a savings of $21,200!

Healthy work lunches can be prepared ahead of time by cooking several large meals in advance and freezing them in individual portions. This way, we have lunch menu choices to pick from.

If we are going out for a group lunch, order something inexpensive. Ask for separate checks for each person. We will save on the tip as well.

How many times a month, do we grab a candy bar, snacks, sodas, or cookies from a vending machine? Add a monthly total. Is the amount enough to bring us down to earth? An alternative, after learning PAA, would be to bring our own bounty from home, such as carrot sticks, homemade cookies, or a piece of fruit.

Do we go out at the end of our workweek to a special bar or restaurant to socialize with coworkers or friends, regardless if we have a nest egg or we owe someone money? Alert! Add up our socializing tab for a month, and then multiply it by twelve. Fifteen dollars a week — that is $780 a year! Of course, we could opt to go out as usual to enjoy the camaraderie, but not spend any money. Or we could suggest a free activity that we could all enjoy instead. Taking advantage of these occasions allows us to save money to increase our financial cushion if we find ourselves unemployed or out of work due to illness.

When possible, live near our business. There's big money saved here. There's no need for a second vehicle if we are married, no extra tires, repairs or extra gasoline needed. We ride a bus or walk. We eliminate the stress and hassle of commuting. We are the winner.

After all is said and done, we could be trimming $10 or more each week from our workplace expenditures, which includes purchasing less expensive clothing, and saving money on gas not used because we carpool. That's $500 a year or more! Eliminate the feeling of deprivation as we cut back. Feel richer.

The money we save in our workplace over the course of a year could pay for our utility bills.

And if we are contemplating a job change, do not quit our job until we find other employment. Even losing a week's wages can result in late rental or vehicle payments.

CHAPTER 17

SCAMS AND CON ARTISTS

There are many varieties of con artists and scammers. We need to be aware and observant. Remember, everyone wants our money. It's up to us to differentiate between a con or scam and an honest deal. This chapter helps us make the distinction.

Cons come in various disguises. A man called us, saying he worked for Sears, and as a store promotion, wanted to clean our furniture, curtains, and rugs. We said "*no*". Then we called Sears and they informed us they had no such promotion! If we had been scam smart in the 1990s we would have gotten a phone number to call them back after we made a decision, and would have called the police instead to report the scam.

Phone solicitors can be swindlers in masquerade that set out to victimize as many unsuspecting people as possible. We have a policy not to purchase in this manner. If we need something, we get estimates and go from there. Also, beware of phone solicitors that mumble messages, talk in heavy accents, and do not talk clearly when explaining exactly what it is they are selling. Seniors are vulnerable targets and can be scammed out of their retirement money and lifetime savings.

If we get calls asking us for personal information, whether it sounds legitimate or not, do not answer any questions: instead ask for a return phone number to call them back. Then call police and give them the number.

Identity thieves love to go through garbage. Do not put anything in the garbage that has personal information, such as our name, address, phone or cell phone numbers, account numbers, statements, any pin numbers, old checks, or expired credit cards. Shred these before throwing them away and cut up credit cards into tiny strips, dividing the pieces between several garbage bags. Guard the privacy of all personal data. Keep wallets and credit cards secured, and vehicles and homes locked. Avoid unsavory neighborhoods that put us in danger of being victimized by crime.

We all have old tax returns that we keep for several years in case we are audited. In the past we might have thrown older bundles of returns away intact. Now we are more prudent. Before discarding returns we shred every paper.

Bank frauds are yet another scary scenario. Someone may call us, saying they are a bank auditor or manager. They'll try to weasel personal data from us, then access our account and abscond with our money. If we receive such a call, ask for a phone number to call them back. Then call our bank and local law enforcement bureau with the information and the phone number. Legitimate bank personnel do not call customers and ask for private information.

Notify the bank immediately before depositing a check in the following instances:

1. From selling big ticket items on the Internet
2. If the check is more than the selling price
3. If we have been instructed to wire excess funds from the check back to the person as soon as possible
4. If the check is from an individual we have communicated with via e-mail
5. If the check is drawn on a business or individual account different from the

name of the person buying our item or product

6. If we have been informed that we were the winner in a Lottery that we did not enter

Bank personnel are trained in determining if we have a legitimate check or if the check could be a fraud.

Cons are in bank parking lots. Always put cash away, out of sight, while still at the teller window. Never exit a bank with money in our hand. If our teller starts counting out our money where others can easily overhear the amount, put our finger up to shush them. In the parking lot of the bank I worked for, a customer's purse was snatched. Upon investigation, we found someone was observing her withdrawal transaction, followed her out and robbed her.

Credit card fraud: Scammers that already have our credit card numbers may call us and try to wheedle out the seven digit number on the back of our card. Do not ever give out this information, unless we are initiating the call. If we are in this situation, ask the caller for a return phone number to call them back. Then call our credit card company and report the fraud and cancel our card. A new one will be issued.

Telemarketer calls can be just as fraudulent. When callers speak in slurred voices, use pressure tactics, ask us to send money for disaster relief, send money up front to receive a product from an unknown company, or call for a local fundraiser, beware. Absolutely do not buy anything from persons that do not speak clearly or that use pressure tactics. If we choose to contribute to disaster relief or a family in need, there are legitimate agencies that are set up to receive our donations. Always research companies before sending them any of our hard earned money. For local fundraisers, call the appropriate company or local Chamber of Commerce to verify the solicitation. When we receive calls to donate to the Police Benevolent association, we take our check to the police department. We do not mail it to an unknown address. Rule of thumb to avoid scams: When we require anything, we are the one that initiates contact.

If someone swears they can do something fabulous for us, something we really want, beware if they ask for money up front. Do not get suckered into this scam. Unsuspecting people have lost millions.

May 2006, our neighbor saw an ad in a magazine proclaiming government land for sale. By sending $20 they mail us a packet with instructions on how to buy these lands for almost no money. I knew immediately it was a scam. To verify it, John and I went to the State Land Management Office. We were indeed told it was a scam. Our local police department gave us the phone number for the Federal Trade Commission, which handles complaints and scams. Their number is 1-877-382-4357.

Sending away for a product from an unknown company could be a con, also. They'll take our money and run. If we need to order from an unknown company, first, check out their credibility.

There are repair frauds in the vehicle and home repair businesses and in other areas. Before hiring anyone or using services from unknown sources, get reliable references. We would not want carpet cleaners or lawn maintenance workers casing our home to return and burglarize it later.

One scam's trick of the trade is to excite us enough to overlook precautions. Be aware of this tactic. Using PAA, we will have the impetus to back down.

A sales pitch: "Quick." "Buy now." "Immediately." "Limited quantities." "Maximum 10 per customer." "These prices are for a short time only — act now!" The psychological scam is to get us to buy ten, when we weren't even aware that we wanted one in the first place.

Supermarkets offer child size carts. We rationalize it's *cute*. Actually, it's a marketing ploy that gets us to spend more money. As we walk through the store, with a budgeted list in hand, our children put whatever they want into their own carts. At checkout the bill is $10.00 more than we intended to spend. Is this still *cute*? The grocery stores rack up more sales and we go into debt.

We order a pizza. They hand us a coupon for a free drink if we order another pizza. Without using PAA, we splurge, thinking we got a good deal.

As promotions and maneuvers that benefit them, credit card companies send blank checks to use and the amount is added to our balance. John and I never use these checks. We shred and toss them away.

Be alert to news programs, e-mails, newspapers, radio, and word of mouth to keep up-to-date on the latest scams. New ones pop up frequently.

Remember, everyone wants our money. Be aware. Take an offensive stand. Hold on to our money like it is life itself. We will never need to say, "If only I had known." PAA's life jacket is here to stay.

CHAPTER 18

UTILITIES

This chapter will give suggestions on how to cut back on laundry techniques, electric, phone, heating, air conditioning, and water usage. It will also emphasize how to conserve energy and save money in the kitchen. Some ideas may seem too minute to bother with, but when they're combined, money savings increase. So armed with PAA, let's get started.

Laundry: We live in an apartment that has pay washers and dryers. Unless there's a schedule, most times when we want them, they're in use. If we are lucky enough to find laundry machines available in our building, it would take a half a day or longer to wash all our loads. The amount of money we need to put into the machines adds up quickly.

Use the lesser amount of soap that the detergent company recommends, unless the load is heavily soiled. I use slightly less soap than is called for and my cloths come out clean.

Use only the amount of water necessary for each load. If a shorter cycle is indicated, use it. The regular cycle need not be used for every type of load. The shorter the cycle, the less electricity is used.

Using cold water for both washing and rinsing saves money, too. I had been raised to use hot water only. I never believed that cold water could clean laundry, but bravery overcame my doubts. I tried it. It worked. Stains are removed or become less set. Hot water tends to set stains.

The only exception is when the clothing label specifically recommends a warm or hot wash.

Do full loads. It's cheaper. It saves detergent, water and electricity. If we need something quickly before a full load is gathered, wash it out by hand. If washing out clothes by hand is beneath us, relax and think PAA. Our success is dependent on our attitude and fortitude. The more money saving ideas we incorporate into our daily routine, the more we benefit.

Wash a load in the evening. Dry it in the morning. There's less moisture but enough to prevent wrinkles. Set the dryer for 10 to 15 minutes less, thereby saving money on electricity. Most items should be dry. The ones that are not: hang them up. They should dry quickly. Use cool tumble cycle instead of the normal hot dry cycle. It doesn't fry dried clothes and, again, uses less electricity. Clothes come out fluffier and the dryer shuts off automatically as it senses the clothes are dry.

Clean lint filters after each load. Proper maintenance cuts down on repairs.

When we run out of detergent and our brand isn't on sale, by all means, buy the detergent that is on sale. We may prefer our brand, but the other brand may do just as well. If not, while we are using the new brand, watch for sales on our brand. But before using it, finish up the other brand.

I was working two jobs, six days and three nights and didn't enjoy spending my only day off doing laundry at my apartment complex. I started doing it every other week and then stretched it to three weeks. Then I started using a commercial Laundromat. The machines were bigger, which allowed me to double up on the loads. I saved on soap and used fewer quarters, but most of all I saved time to relax. I spent about two and a half hours from start to finish instead of an entire day.

Laundry and clothes drying: Towels with thick pile take up excessive room in the washing machine and take longer to dry, costing more in electric bills or using more quarters in a commercial facility.

Some fabric softener sheets can be used twice. Try different brands.

Immediately remove clothes from the dryer when the cycle ends. The clothes are less wrinkled. We will save ironing, time, and electricity.

Before the invention of clothes dryers, laundered clothes were hung outside on clotheslines. In inclement weather, they were hung in garages, porches or inside. "Yuck", we say. "I will not regress back to the Dark Ages." Remember PAA. Even if we won't give up our dryer entirely, try hanging up just one or two loads every washday. For those who don't have yards, purchase a retractable wall mounted clothesline for our home. There are other options, such as a folding wooden or metal drying rack.

Two or three times a year check the dryer exhaust pipes to make sure they are clear of dust and lint. It's a fire preventative measure and it helps with the working efficiency of the dryer.

ELECTRIC

Electric rates have soared. Are we going to let the electric companies get away with this? NO! Let's show them they are not getting any more of our money unnecessarily.

Make our home as airtight as possible. Caulk. Insulate. Seal. Make sure windows and doors are tightly shut. Ask our electric company for an energy analysis. It's often free. It finds air leaks around doors, windows, floors and ceilings. It could save us extraordinary amounts of money in heat and air conditioning bills. Ask our electric company if it offers incentives for purchasing energy savings appliances. We received a $60 check from our electric company for buying an energy efficient hot water heater.

Fluorescent and energy saver bulbs use less wattage and last longer than standard bulbs.

Lighting fixtures. Purchase ones that use normal size bulbs, not specialty bulbs that cost more to replace.

Light bulbs may emit heat. In warm weather, reduce the light source close to us and near the air conditioning thermostat. The opposite is true in colder weather. For instance, bathroom light bulbs could produce enough warmth to reduce the heat thermostat several degrees.

If we feel chilly at home, don't go to raise the thermostat. Go for our favorite robe.

In air conditioning months, we raise the thermostat several degrees, dress cooler and use fans. In the winter months, we set the thermostat to 60 degrees. We dress a little warmer. It saves a lot on electric bills.

Some electric companies offer a budget payment plan where the electric usage is averaged out over a period of a year. The payments are usually the same every month with some adjustments made as needed.

Always turn lights off when leaving a room and turn computers off when not in use.

When purchasing appliances, choose energy efficient brands. The small extra costs are made up and then some within a few years.

We close off the rooms we seldom use, turning thermostats off or reducing them.

Keep furnaces and other heat sources clean and in good repair. It saves electricity, gas, and costs of replacement.

Use dimmer switches wherever possible. It uses less wattage.

Make sure the fireplace damper is closed when it's not in use.

Use fans to offset heating and air conditioning bills.

Reduce the hot water heater temperature to 115 or 120 degrees. Yes, it is adequate.

John insulated our water pipes for protection against winter freezing and installed an insulated blanket on the water heater.

Some people wash their hair every day, either because it's oily, or they just feel it needs frequent washings. Try changing shampoos. Find one that leaves our hair looking and reacting better. We may be able to cut back on daily washings, which will save on electricity, hot water costs, and shampoo costs. Drying hair with an electric hair blower gobbles up electricity as well. Every day that hair doesn't need washing is just that more money saved.

When building a new home, explore all the new energy savings technologies. Solar heating, underground heat sources and floor heat are just a few.

Use weather striping where necessary. The dollars used for these materials are far less than the excess energy burned and lost due to cracks around windows, doors, fireplaces, attics and roofs.

Some of the highest costs of electricity are from clothes dryers, dishwashers, heating and air conditioning, freezers, water heating, ovens and refrigerators. These areas are worth thoughts and strategies to cut back wherever possible. Again, think PAA.

Close freezer and refrigerator doors tightly. Use the least amount of time for drying clothes. Use full loads in the dishwasher. Do not preheat oven before needed.

We have total control over the electric bill. There are choices to consider:

Long showers versus short showers: The longer the shower, the more water and electricity are used. We do not need bathtubs full of water; all that is required is just enough water to bathe. Also, cut back on the water temperature a bit.

Working appliances that stay plugged in are always turning the electric meter, such as clocks, humidifiers, freezers, refrigerators, fans, hot water tanks, heaters and air conditioners, computers, VCRs, and fish tanks. Before leaving home, decide which ones to unplug.

Over all, we tend to use electricity indiscriminately, without thinking about the consequences. For instance, the electric meter running all day on the television set, whether it's being watched or not, and washing clothes or dishes with half full loads.

By using PAA, the electric entry on our budget could very well be listed on the fixed expenditures instead of the fluctuating expenditure column. It is possible, by awareness, to keep electricity usage at a reasonable level.

John and I live in an area of cool nights and warm days. In the summer, we close the windows in the morning, preserving the cool air throughout the day. At night the windows are open. According to where the sun is positioned during the day, we close the curtains to prevent the sun from warming the house. Later in the day, we close the curtains on the opposite side, and reopen the others.

On winter nights, we turn down the heat thermostats to 40 to 50 degrees for about eight hours.

WATER

I believe, as Americans, we have a responsibility to preserve natural resources. If our help comes in the form of reporting corporations that pollute or just from cutting back on water usage, each little bit counts. To clean up polluted waterways, oceans, lakes and rivers, our tax monies are used. Less pollution equals fewer taxes paid. We save money. Water pollutants can seep into drinking water. We then need to buy bottled water. We don't save here.

Some suggestions for saving water:

1. When washing clothes, use only the amount of water needed for that size load.
2. When washing items in the sink, turn the water off until all items are ready to rinse.
3. Quickies in the kitchen sink: When using water from a faucet for just a moment, use cold water. Placing it in the hot position uses energy to heat water that never reaches the faucet.
4. Every bit of hot water not used reduces the energy needed to heat hot water in the hot water tank.
5. While brushing teeth, shaving or taking a shower, turn the water off until rinsing time.
6. Showers and baths: Use a bit cooler water temperature and a shorter time in the shower. Install flow restricted showerheads, faucets, and commodes.
7. Water lawns at night. Daytime heat and sun quickly evaporate water.

TELEPHONES

There's lots of ways to save money on phones. Many people do not have regular phones in their homes anymore. They rely solely on cell phones, and depending on the plan, we can save lots of money.

For those with regular phones in the house, they have options of including long distance with their phone company or to use the phone for local calls only. Having a phone card for long distance can save big dollars, thus eliminating a long distance carrier altogether. Long distance calls, then, are made from cell phones, phone cards, even on computers. Shop around for the best plan for our particular needs. There's a plan out there for everyone.

Some phone cards let us know how many minutes are still available before the call is put through. When minutes are running low, we call customer service and have more minutes added. This is a true convenience. At the time this book was written, phone card rates were as low as 2.7 cents a minute with no connection charges. That's less than paying a fixed rate of $40 or more per month for a cell phone, or paying higher long distance rates through our phone company.

However, if we use long distance as a working tool, it may be cheaper to pay the cell phone fixed rate. Even $60 or $70 a month could be a bargain.

Look for hidden costs on any phone service (home, cell, or card) and weigh them first before committing to one particular service.

Dialing information: Use it only as a last resort. Look up the number needed in the phone book or the Internet.

Collect calls are very expensive. Use for emergency only.

PAYING UTILITY BILLS

When feasible, take payments directly to the company or use drop boxes, which are usually located in selected stores near us. With postage rates increasing, here is a way to save: Get together with friends, neighbors, or colleagues. Send all the bills in one envelope. Make sure the checks are attached to the proper bills. Those owning a computer can pay bills online.

ON VACATION

1. Turn thermostats at a lower setting in winter and a higher setting in summer.
2. Turn the hot water heater off, or lower in the winter.
3. Use a light timer instead of leaving lights on continuously.
4. Unplug lights and appliances.

The U.S. Department of Energy has a useful brochure on energy savers. Go to www.doe.gov and click on Energy Savers or http://www.eere.energy.gov/consumer/.

KITCHEN

All appliances: Buy appliances that are energy efficient, and fit our needs, not the ones that have extras that we will never use.

Fill dishwashers to full capacity. Prior to turning it on, run sink hot water for a minute. This saves dishwasher energy. The water is already hot. The dishwasher does not need to heat the water as much.

Use a smaller oven to prepare little servings, such as a toaster oven. It keeps the house cooler and uses less electricity.

While cooking: Covering pots until the contents boil uses less electricity and heats up faster. As contents begin to boil, turn the temperature down. It still boils but it saves on electricity or gas.

Dishes. One set suffices. If we wish to invest in an extra set for special occasions or company, that's fine, as long as the purchase fits into our budget. However, buying china for specialty holidays could be listed as an extravagance if we are on a limited budget. Food tastes the same whether served on everyday china or holiday china.

China manufacturers have come out with a variety of dishes for specific foods. To name a few: popcorn, chili, soup, corn on the cob, cereal, platters for fish and poultry. We don't *need* any of these. All of these foods can be served on the dishes that we already possess.

Cut down on paper towel use. I bought a ten pack of washcloths for $5. I use them everywhere I used paper towels. My paper towel bills shrunk. The cost of the washcloths has paid for itself time and again. Used paper towels are thrown out. Used washcloths are washed and used again.

Better grade paper napkins cost more than the economy lower grade napkins. I purchase the most for the least amount of money. They are thrown away anyway.

I needed an extra large mixing bowl. Most of the stainless steel bowls came in sets. I found a single one with a slight dent. I ask for and received a discount. It was more cost effective for the store. They didn't have to pay to ship it back to the manufacturer. It works as well as any bowl without a dent.

Cleaning compounds. Use white vinegar for almost everything. It's much cheaper than using different specialty cleaners to clean each thing. Read the label for instructions.

Kitchen garbage. Completely fill the bags before discarding. Break up food packaging containers into flat pieces to save space. Money is saved on garbage bags.

Opening freezer and refrigerator doors lets in warmer air. It takes these appliances a while to cool the air. Before opening the doors, have a plan. Take out everything needed for a complete meal. Then put everything away at once after the meal. The doors were only open twice, instead of multiple times; for instance, it would be a waste of power to open the refrigerator door for orange juice, then fruit, then milk, then bread, butter and jelly.

When purchasing new sets of cookware, buy the best we can afford. This is a good investment. Less expensive sets can warp, the non-stick finish can wear off, and knobs on pot covers can loosen. It's cheaper in the long run to have a good set.

Are we baking? Time the baking completion with the onset of starting a meal as the oven is already hot.

Use kitchen ventilation fans sparingly. They quickly suck up warm or cool air out of our home.

Take care of what we have. Follow the manufacturers' care procedures. Pouring hot water into a cold pot or placing cold water in a pot could warp them. Cutting foods in a pot damages the surface. What is well cared for won't need replacing. Money is saved.

CHAPTER RECAP

We must ask ourselves how many ways we can spend less and save more. Make a list. Act on it.

Use less of everything. Lower and raise thermostats, use cooler water, set dryer times shorter, use appliances less for shorter periods of time.

Saving little bits here and there adds up.

By using PAA we can do these things. From here on, Joe Blow will not be getting any more of our money than is necessary.

CHAPTER 19

VACATION AND TRAVEL

This chapter will show us how to incorporate PAA into our travel plans and activities, while saving money, and still enjoy doing it.

If we are planning to fly, the most important thing is the ticket cost. First class is a luxurious way to fly. The seats are more comfortable, and the service and meals are better than coach service. If we want to save money, go coach. If the reason for flying first class is an ego builder, think of it as throwing college tuition or retirement money down the drain. Exercise PAA.

Flying coach may entail airline cutbacks on meals and seat comfort. When we fly, we pack our own healthy meals and snacks and devour them while others have peanut snacks. We request aisle seats, which gives us extra legroom. We don't fuss about the inconvenience. We arrive at our destination at the same time as first class, but pay less for tickets. The money saved by flying coach gives us more spending money for the vacation.

Getting the tickets at the best price is challenging. There are ways to cut down on expense. Call many travel agencies to compare prices. Go to airline offices for comparison. The Internet offers many avenues to save money, as well. Call and inquire several times a week at the same locales. The prices fluctuate. To do this, we need a plan in advance. The closer it is to the time of travel, the more expensive the tickets. However, if planes are not full, cheaper fares may be available right before departure dates.

It's also challenging, price wise, if we plan on renting a vehicle. There's much to consider. Always ask for a total price quote, including all the extra charges and taxes. Only purchase insurance if our own company doesn't cover the rental. Inquire what rates are available during weekdays and or weekends. Ask about per mile charges, and the penalty for exceeding the maximum. Some people may rent an expensive vehicle to feed their self-gratification. When we practice PAA, naturally we rent a less expensive vehicle. The money saved could go toward spending more on the vacation or we could save the money.

Motels. Motels situated on highway exits usually cost more than older motels that are off the beaten path. If traveling by vehicle, plan so that if a motel is needed, we will be in a large enough area to find an older mom and pop motel. The amenities may be less than a larger franchised name motel, but a comfortable bed and a good night's sleep give the same feeling of well-being, no matter what the cost.

Gasoline. Plan ahead. The bigger the municipality or city, the more likely gasoline prices will fluctuate. Even in our small area, at times, gasoline prices fluctuate fifteen cents a gallon. We, of course, go to the cheapest. When we are out in the boonies, we expect to pay premium prices. On a trip to the southwest, we found ourselves weaving in and out of California, where gasoline prices are quite high. When it came time to gas up, we'd always be close enough to the border to get cheaper gas in a neighboring state.

Scenario: John and I drove through British Columbia, the Yukon, and Alaska for 19 days. Before leaving, we built a mattress platform inside the covered back of our truck. Under the platform was room for our suitcases, first aid kit, fishing supplies, extra shoes and raingear. Everything had a rope attached to it, so when we needed something, it was easy to pull the rope of the needed item. We put food in a box and ice cooler which fit at the foot of the platform. At night we transferred the food to the truck cab. In the 19 days on the road, we bought food supplies in supermarkets, stayed in one motel, and one campground. The other nights were spent under the stars where we witnessed spectacular panoramas of northern lights changing colors as they danced and flowed across the dark skies.

We cooked our meals on a campfire and enjoyed birds as they dove down and took bites out of our cooking food. They also ate out of our hands. One bird decided to taste our oatmeal as it boiled. He flew from the pot faster than a streak of lightening, with a burned tongue in tow. Squirrels would briskly snatch at the paper towel roll and abscond with it, unraveling it behind them. For showers, we stopped at truck stop service stations. All in all, except for two nights of paid accommodations, the total cost of the trip was for gasoline. We eat regardless of where we're at, so food costs were not added to the overall cost of the trip. We enjoyed this cost saving trip immensely and saw things we'd never have experienced if we had been on a tour, or stayed at motels and ate at restaurants.

Tenting and camping out can be just as rewarding as our truck trip. By conversing with other campers we can exchange foods and get ideas on other sights to visit. The beauty of nature can make lifelong memories. We have picked wild berries and mushrooms and have seen chipmunks, deer, elk, and birds. It's an enjoyable circus just watching the animals. Camping out is less costly than staying at motels and buying meals.

Traveling by trailer or using an R.V. is a great way to travel if we do it often enough to offset the large up front expenditure. It's great having our own facilities at our disposal. But, before investing in such expensive purchases, think of how often it will be used, its resale value, and fuel costs.

There are thousands of used R.V. and trailer dealerships. When purchasing one, deciding on length, maneuverability, amenities, and gasoline mileage is of utmost importance. Remember, the smaller it is, the more money saved. If it is being financed, the higher the loan, the more interest charged. Be sure this type of travel is what we really want. Money can be lost in resale.

Train travel can be just as expensive as flying. There are pros and cons. The train offers the opportunity to view beautiful landscapes, and talk with others from around the world. However, there are often delays, "meals" are outrageously expensive and sleepers are out of financial range for many travelers. Seats are not as comfortable to sleep in as beds are. If we do travel by train, bring as many homemade meals as we can. We have a choice on food: theirs or ours. Use our life preserver, PAA, and save money.

While visiting anywhere, go where the natives go: motels, restaurants, supermarkets, and gift shops. They're cheaper than resorts, beachfront, mountain get-a-ways, or tourist attractions.

The great American marketing machine cannot wait to reel us in when we shop for vacation clothes. Ever since I was a child, there have been mega advertising programs telling us we need *vacation clothes.* It was a given. We were programmed. Vacation and new clothes were synonymous. We flocked to stores to buy the latest in vacation wear, be it sailing clothes, coordinating three-piece, light weight outfits, or special walking shoes. Price was not paramount; the new clothes to fit the vacation were.

Enter PAA. Nowhere is it written in stone that having fun-filled vacations is directly associated with having a new wardrobe. Let's stop being fish that are scooped up in the marketing machine's propaganda. Let's wear what we have. Save the money not spent. Deposit it into our IRA account.

Be discriminating. Carefully choose what attractions are worth the admission price. This is entirely an individual decision. We saved $16 by not going on a castle tour. Instead, we bought a few postcards of the inside and meandered through the beautiful outside gardens. But if castles are our big interest, then go for the entrance fee and cut back on something else.

Go where the natives go, not where the tourists go (restaurants, entertainment, shopping, gift stores). They are cheaper and save us gobs of money.

Plan ahead on travel needs. Cameras need batteries and film. If we live in an area that has discount stores, buy plenty of film and extra batteries before leaving home. We were caught short on film when we visited Denali National Park in Alaska. Paying $8.00 per roll of film was discouraging, when we could have bought eight rolls for the same money before leaving home.

When developing film back home, shop around for the best prices. Of course, if we have digital cameras there is no developing required.

We stopped at a pay phone to call a cousin. The charge was 25 cents per minute. We beat the system. We went to a motel, asked if we could use their phone for a couple of minutes and they said, "yes." All of us can use our imagination to improvise money saving techniques.

Avoid toll roads if at all possible. The free roads are usually more scenic and have points of interest to whet our appetite for unusual new adventures.

Before traveling by vehicle, invest in a cooler. Buy foods at supermarkets. Make our own meals. Having a picnic by a river's edge that's covered with wildflowers is a nicer setting than any restaurant, unless, of course, it's raining.

As in the workplace, if we do go to a restaurant while on vacation, order an inexpensive meal. It fills us up the same as a more costly meal, and we save money both on the meal and on the tip. Or order take-out.

Snacks cost more from a vending machine than if purchased at a discount store. Having a banana or an apple instead of a vending machine snack also saves money.

Do we ever get a yen for a certain food while traveling? If it's a bagel we crave, it costs about 80 cents. If we want a spread on it, the price goes way up. We just buy a bagel, scavenge our cooler and make our own toppings. It's fun.

Pack light. It costs less in clothes purchases and saves gas. Have we ever seen someone overloaded with heavy luggage? Half the contents come home without leaving the suitcase. If we travel frequently, choose several three-piece coordinating outfits made from easy to clean fabrics. That's all we need besides accessories. It's cheaper on luggage size, clothes, and better on our purse and our back.

Some credit card companies offer free flyer miles as an incentive to use their credit card. This is fine, as long as we don't charge more than we can pay off in full when the bill comes.

If our vacation budget is too small to travel to distant places, opt to stay at home, making short day trips to see sights around our state. For instance, visit historical sites, free museums and galleries, go on a hike at a new place, and make supper picnics to eat at our favorite park. Ask our local Chamber of Commerce for listings of attractions in our area.

A few important points worth remembering:

1. Do not go into debt when vacationing or traveling.
2. Just because many people go to a certain vacation spot, doesn't mean we

need to catch a coattail and follow. Some people are paying off vacationing debt for many years. Imagine the interest paid on that debt.

3. Purchase necessities before leaving home. It saves us lots of money.
4. Buy food at supermarkets.
5. Always check and compare prices for the best deal, no matter where we go.

CHAPTER 20

VEHICLES

Do we need a new vehicle? Remember that vehicle commercials and ads try to get us excited. The smiles, fast talk, and beautiful scenery are not important facts to consider. What we should be interested in is performance, fuel efficiency, miles per gallon, a price we can "easily" afford, and comfort. Think carefully before adding extras. They have a tendency to cost above what we are willing to pay. The vehicle should fit our needs and not the dealership's need to meet a quota.

Look at all possible areas that offer vehicles for sale. Check ads, the Internet, ask around, and go to both used and new vehicle lots. A used car lot might have the car we are looking for. Many people trade in or sell almost new vehicles when they receive company vehicles, move, or are pressed for money.

Are we out to impress others with our new vehicle? Do we have a need to live up to the Jones's? Do we have an attitude that purchasing an expensive or flashy vehicle feeds our ego and makes us a better person? If we are a millionaire, that's OK. But otherwise, it's not. There are so many ways to use and save that money for necessities. Why squander it on an ego driven want, when we can be building a new positive financial goal? Our disposition will either land us in debt or save us from debt. The choice is ours.

Avoid making hasty decisions. I once bought a new model car the first year it came out. It was a lemon. Models that have good track records and have proven to be trustworthy are better choices.

Keep checking around, again and again. We may get the price reduced. Tell the dealership we have X amount of money to spend, and no more. Always say we have less money than we do. Then we will have a leeway for extras. Find out what the monthly payments are and make sure they are affordable. The dealership wants to make a sale. They may come down in price. Remember, it's no sin to haggle.

John and Judy's Scenario: In 1999, our decrepit, wobbly ten-year-old truck had 189,000 miles and it needed to be replaced. We compared prices at two dealerships in our area. New trucks were expensive. We checked out every used vehicle lot and came across one that purchased almost new vehicles from Canada. We saved $6,000 off the new priced trucks. The truck had 4,500 miles on it and was manufactured in the US. Other than regular maintenance, we've had no other expenses. A portion of the price difference was the Canadian rate of exchange at the time. Was the deal as easy as walking into a new car dealership? No. We looked for several months. We found that the smaller lots had less overhead expenses than bigger national name lots, therefore, their prices were more reasonable. The difference of the $6,500 savings enabled us to pay cash instead of financing payments and paying interest.

We kept within our budget. If it had meant buying an older truck, we would have done that, as well. We do not need to impress anyone. What we needed was reliable transportation and to know that our truck purchase would not put us in debt.

John and I purchased an almost new travel trailer. We saved $3,000. Between buying the truck and trailer we saved $9,500. This is a perfect example of how John maintained financial astuteness over the years.

Finding a good used vehicle can be challenging. Take the same route as we would to buy a new vehicle. Some people still prefer to trade in their vehicles every three years. So, we can get good deals as long as we do our homework before buying. Keep price in mind, as well as odometer readings and fuel efficiency. Before making the sale final, take the used vehicle to a diagnostic center. It could save us money in the long run. Check the tires for wear.

If a used vehicle needs repairs, ask if repair costs are the responsibility of the seller or the buyer. It should be up to the seller to repair the vehicle before we buy it. When my son purchased a used vehicle, the dealership sent the car through a diagnostic test, where they found a few problems. They immediately repaired everything before the sale was finalized.

However, if we have to pay the cost, make sure that it fits into our budget. If not, ask that the sale price be reduced in an amount that is commensurate with the cost of repairs. It's better to be overly cautious before purchasing than to be financially strapped with repairs or worse later on. Go to as many used vehicle outlets as we can to compare, investigate, research and haggle prices. The dealerships always want to make sales and most are willing to work with us. This is no time to be shy or complacent.

As with any vehicle, having maintenance and repair knowledge can save oodles of money. The more knowledge we have, the fewer times we need to pay for service and repairs. Buying the needed new part and delivering it to the repair shop also reduces the total cost.

When new expensive parts are needed for repairs, ask about rebuilt or used parts. There are pros and cons here: how long those parts will last, how long we intend to keep the vehicle, and if performance will be as good as a new part, etc.

When we needed a new motor for our truck, we bought a rebuilt one and saved $3,000. It's working just like a new one.

We needed a new tailgate for our old truck.. New ones were expensive. We found an almost new one at a junkyard and installed it ourselves for a fraction of the cost of a new one. We saved $300.

Scenario: A new car is $20,000, with interest free payments for three years. By offering cash, the price will likely be reduced. The dealership doesn't lose money by offering free financing. The interest money may have been figured into the original asking price.

VEHICLE MAINTENANCE

Before choosing a maintenance or repair shop, ask friends, family, or coworkers for references. Then call several for price comparisons, hours of service, charges per hour, labor and any other hidden charges. One repair shop we went to charged us for a full hour for labor, even though the work was finished in forty-five minutes. They lost a customer.

We needed a maintenance job on our truck. The dealership's price was $150. The other two places we received estimates were $99 and $75 for the same work.

We have choices to make. Some maintenance things are worth paying the higher price; some are not. It's our decision. We went to the cheapest facility.

Purchase vehicle oil by the case when it's on sale. Keep maintenance current, including proper air pressure in the tires. Drive the vehicle as long as we can, banking the amount of the payments after it's been paid off. Try saving enough for a good down payment on our next vehicle. We will save both on interest and a shortened length of payment time.

For the handicapped person, full service gasoline and hood checks are a great convenience. But for the rest of us, the self-service is the cheaper way to go.

There are many service stations in our area. Their prices widely fluctuate by as much as eighteen cents a gallon. Before PAA some people would say, "What the heck? It's only pennies." After learning PAA the same person would go to the cheapest station.

With gasoline prices so high, here are some ways to cut back:

1. Conserve gas by going on errands in a straight path, instead of backtracking. Do as many errands as possible at one time.
2. Carpool whenever possible.
3. Walk instead of driving. Use a bicycle or bus.
4. Drive slower on highways. Besides saving on gas, it also saves peace of mind.
5. Use less traveled routes. We save time and gas from not sitting idle in traffic.
6. Drive free of radios, air conditioning and heat wherever possible. These use gas energy.
7. Drive as smoothly as possible without braking or accelerating. Use cruise control.
8. Timely vehicle maintenance protects against unnecessary repairs and improves gas mileage.
9. Avoid rush hour traffic, too much idling, starts, and stops.
10. Proper tire air pressure extends mileage.
11. Bigger vehicles, pickup trucks, and SUVs may be fun but hybrids and

smaller cars are more fuel-efficient.
PAA works well here.

Everywhere, drive conservatively. Go slower around turns and curves. It saves on tire wear. The self-gratification attitude will ignore these suggestions and go as fast as they can. They will buy more tires more often in the long run. PAA attitude is the winner. Tires are not cheap.

Obey all traffic laws. Tickets are costly and insurance premiums go up after so many tickets. Having a clean driving record reduces insurance premiums. Taking a driver's education class can also reduce vehicle insurance.

After retiring, John worked at a Montana State Park for ten summers, saving every penny. We bought two real estate lots. In another year or two, (prices are escalating), we plan to sell them. Using the profits only, we will purchase a hybrid, fuel efficiency vehicle or an electric vehicle. We will reinvest the principal in other properties. This is what positive attitude adjustment accomplishes.

Scenario: We have just moved into a new home. Shortly afterwards, our vehicle goes on the bum. We are inundated with expenses. PAA in us tells us to buy an inexpensive but stable used vehicle until finances level off. Drive the vehicle until enough is saved for a sizable down payment on a better vehicle. Values of homes usually increase. Vehicle values usually depreciate.

Scenario: Through the media and advertisements we are told to buy new vehicles and finance them over a period of so many years. The wise person drives an old car until enough money has been saved to purchase a better one.

No matter what our income, many families own two or more vehicles. A family of two may own four vehicles. The costs not only include the vehicles, but four registrations, four insurance policies, four maintenances, and quadruple amounts for tires. It's expensive, to say the least.

There are families that have two adults working in opposite sections of town. They each need a vehicle. But figure it out first. Does the price for the second vehicle warrant the income derived? The decision should include costs of insurance, registration, fuel, and maintenance. Is one job's location accessible by bus? Is it possible to get a job closer to the other person's job? Is it possible for one to carpool? One vehicle is still a lot cheaper than two.

John and I have one vehicle and with a little give and take, there's no problem. We work around appointments and activities and save thousands a year.

SAVING MONEY IN OTHER AREAS TO USE TOWARDS GASOLINE

The cost of gas has increased tremendously over the last several years. If we cut back on our other purchases, we can apply the money that we save towards higher fuel costs.

Scenario: John and I take a multivitamin every day at a monthly cost of $10.00. A friend suggested we switch to her multivitamin brand, which has more nutriments, at a cost of $25.00 a month. After we compared his brand to ours and gave it consideration, and taking into account that we already eat a healthful fare, we decided to keep using our brand. With the cost of gasoline escalating, the $15.00 a month we save, by not purchasing the more expensive vitamins, will go toward paying for gas. We can personalize this scenario to suit a host of other situations.

ROAD RAGE

Two areas that I have mentioned previously that we can practice PAA are our diets and in the workplace. It can also help to curb road rage. The financial denominator for road rage is that it puts wear and tear on our vehicles, and produces stress and anxiety, therefore, costing money.

The new mindset to help prevent road rage is to think that other people do not perform outrageous maneuvers in their cars to disturb us as individuals, but rather because they are upset or angry about something that happened to them personally, or they just do things behind the wheel without looking or thinking. If those who practice road rage used PAA, they would discover the reasons they overreact when driving (as in overspending). This would allow them to meet these reasons head-on, develop a new approach to act differently, and affect a lasting change in their behavior.

CHAPTER 21

HODGEPODGE

This chapter covers the odds and ends that were not included in previous chapters, but are important just as well.

Housing: Always buy beneath our budgeted income. Taxes go up, repairs are needed, and emergencies arise. Many of us purchase a home above our means. Loving the home far outweighs rationality. While we finagle and fudge financial records so we can move into the house, it doesn't enter our minds that we are hurting no one but ourselves. Not until after we move in, does our bad judgment hit us like a ton of bricks. By then, it's too late. Financial instability begins to snowball. Once we get in the habit of living beyond our means, we are debt destined.

After learning about PAA we get smarter. We realize. We don't rationalize. Instead of purchasing everything just slightly above our means, we begin to buy things below our means. We save the difference. We remain debt-free.

Are we buying a first home? Buy a duplex instead. John did. He lived in one side and rented the other. The rental money covered his mortgage payment, taxes, and insurance. He saved the monthly payments, just as if he were paying rent. He invested the money by purchasing property, holding on to it for a couple of years, and then reselling it for a profit. He would not have considered dwindling his assets by acquiring inconsequential possessions. John chose to use the profits to build our home. He also could have chosen to buy another duplex for increased income.

Tip: When purchasing real estate, a home, or business, remember location, location, and location. We may love the property, home, or business, but think of it as a resale possibility.

Buying homes above our means does not guarantee a happier existence. We can rationalize we will be getting raises which means we will be able to afford the home. But raises may not materialize, a job may be lost, or an illness could cause extended unemployment. We may also think we can afford the mortgage payment, yet not consider if we can afford it plus insurance and taxes. I have seen the results of buying above our means and more times than not, it develops into a nightmare of debt where homes are foreclosed, wages are garnished, and owners are ruined financially for years to come.

Home repairs: Prepare ahead of time by learning how to make our own repairs. Call professional repair people only when we have repairs that we are not qualified to make. Hire our own help. It's cheaper than contracting it out. Friends of ours were building a home. The builder paid a worker $7.00 an hour to clean up the construction debris. The builder charged the owner $18 an hour. The builder pocketed the $11 an hour difference.

Maintain everything: windows, lawnmowers, gutters, clothes dryers, tractors, saws, refrigerators, freezers, roofs, and all other machines and appliances. Read manuals and follow maintenance instructions. Preserving what we have will save us money in the long run by not having repair bills.

When we buy a smaller, cheaper home beneath our income, we save in more ways than a reduced mortgage payment. Our taxes, insurance, utility and maintenance bills are less and we save money on furnishings. Haunt secondhand furniture stores and go to home auctions. Call several home decorator services and ask them where they sell their rejects (special order furniture that comes in with flaws). In Hollywood, Florida, there was a store that carried decorator rejects for a fraction of retail price. I bought a sofa for $100 that had a pin size snag on the back that originally sold for $1,000. The matching chair, which had a flaw under the armrest, cost $65, which, if in perfect shape, would have sold for $350.

When we need furniture, there are choices to be made that we were not aware of before PAA came into our life. In the past, we naturally went to retail furniture stores. Now, we still go to retail stores, but just to get prices. Then we go to discount outlets and secondhand stores where we have bargaining power. At the retail store, we priced a dining room set for $1,000. The discount outlet had a set for $700. The secondhand store had a beautiful set for $700 but after we bargained, we paid $575. We consumers have the ammunition and money to haggle for the best price at the store of our choice. We need to take advantage of this power.

Home improvements: No matter what the improvements entail, ask ourselves (use our imagination) how many ways we can save money and still have quality. Thinking about it doesn't happen in a day. Give it a while for money saving ideas to come to mind. Then make the final decisions based on the information at hand. For instance, do we want rock included in the landscaping? Look through normal channels first and get estimates. Then look for the out-of-the-way sources. We could get them cheaper or even free.

The same cost effective solutions for homes can be applied to rental apartments. By renting smaller, less expensive apartments, we save across the board: in electric bills, we use less furniture, and we physically save the difference. If we know we are staying in the same location, ask our landlord for a discounted rate for signing an extended lease.

Recycle manila envelopes. Make new labels and tape them over old ones. We haven't bought manila envelopes in years.

Haircuts: Cut it a bit shorter during each haircut. Extend our next cut an extra week. Using PAA allows us to enjoy the extra length. Eliminate complaining. It's to our benefit. We save money.

While writing this book, I kept miniature paper pads in every room of the house. When ideas came, I'd jot them down. While walking for exercise, I wore a pen on a rope around my neck and a pad of paper in my pocket. It was a good system. Most ideas came to me while walking. The pads cost 25 cents each. The pen was $2.00. A friend suggested I buy a miniature hand-held recorder, which would make taking notes easier. I compared prices from several stores. The cheapest one was $24. Even if I had not been writing this book, I'd have kept the pens and pads. The cost wasn't worth the convenience. It would be a purchase I would use for awhile, and then put into storage. However, if we are in business or other areas that the recorder would be used on a regular basis, then, by all means, invest in one.

Merchandise in tube containers: When we think we have finished the contents, cut the tube in thirds, crosswise. Each section still has usable amounts. Store the sections in zip lock bags and enjoy using the rest of the contents a little longer. The cosmetic company I use, puts their moisturizer in tubes. If too much is squeezed out, it is wasted. When I thought the tube was empty, I cut it into thirds. There was enough moisturizer left for another three months! Even with a new tube of product, I transfer the contents into an empty jar or plastic container. This allows me to use only the amount of product I need, never having to waste any because too much came out. Doing just this one thing saves me over $40 a year! By the way, this moisturizer used to come in plastic jars. Could it be that the company decided to change the packaging in order to make more money? If this were true the customer would need to purchase the product more often, without being made aware of the waste that remains in the tube from the new packaging. We need to recognize these underhanded marketing strategies and act accordingly. The cosmetic company has excellent quality products, but I have learned how to get the most out of the products for money spent.

When boxed packages arrive in the mail, save the boxes. Use them again. Buying boxes is not a necessary expenditure.

A friend of ours got an estimate of $6,000 from a contractor to build a garage. He and a friend built it for $3,000.

Take extra good care of our possessions. They'll last longer, saving us replacement costs.

Are we starting out on our own? Share an apartment and utilities. Bank the money we save by sharing expenses. After saving enough money, then go out on our own.

Instead of calling long distance, write a letter or e-mail.

Know the amount of liquid assets we have, live within them, and preferably, below them.

Instead of buying a bike or motorcycle, go for a walk or jog.

Do we need a big-ticket item, when the existing one still gives us somewhat of service? Continue using it until we save enough to pay cash for a new one. The interest paid on credit card purchases will be non-existent and our savings will sigh in relief.

On this same subject, be aware of putting repair after repair into something no longer worth repairing. It might be cheaper in the long run to just get a new one.

Share the expense of subscriptions to newspapers and magazines with friends or neighbors. The only drawback to sharing a newspaper is how to split coupons. With a little compromise, the pros will outweigh the cons. Taking advantage of sales in a newspaper will pay for the cost of the paper. Read newspapers online. Share tools, fixer uppers, services, and hobbies, as well.

Save receipts and all warrantees. No kidding! Stash them in an envelope or make a file for them, but save them! If a product is flawed, or we wish to return it, having the receipt will make it a lot easier. We were robbed of about $3,500 worth of merchandise. I had all the receipts. And, yes, it was a lot easier!

Mosquito bites: Use a dab of household ammonia on a Q-tip and dab the bite with it. It takes the itch right out. It's much cheaper than store bought remedies. We find that ammonia is less drying than alcohol, which does the same job.

A photographer decided to make extra money. From a helicopter, he took aerial photographs of homes in our neighborhood. Then, showing enthusiasm, he came to our home, asking if we'd like to buy the picture of ours. The pictures had all been enlarged and framed. The asking price was $350. I began to wonder what purpose and reason there was for us to purchase it. It was totally out of our realm to even think about such a thing. We decided against the purchase, which immediately changed the demeanor of the photographer to that of disbelief. He reduced the price to $250 to persuade us to buy our picture. He still could not change our minds. We were firm. We wouldn't jeopardize our financial stance just because he decided to take the picture. This was another way we exercised PAA. We were not being cheap. We were being prudent by grabbing hold of the life preserver!

Relationships: Make it clear who pays for what, in the beginning. It can be 50-50 or 100% on one part or anything in between. Be prepared to uphold our end. Learn to say “no”, “I cannot pay for…” or “I cannot repay…” If we need to borrow money, lay down the ground rules first regarding repayment. Bring it out in the open. Do not assume anything. Of course, if we had been practicing PAA, there would be no reason to borrow money.

Hardware stores: We ask for a three-foot piece of lumber. It costs $6.49. Next to it is an eight-foot piece on sale for $6.39. The salesperson may or may not volunteer this information. Keep our eyes open and ask questions.

Many store items come in multiple packs. The same item may be in a single pack. Don’t assume that the multiple packs are cheaper. Check the price difference.

Some stores offer personal accounts. If we open this type of account, ask if there’s a 5% or 10% discount if we pay the bill in full within the first ten days of the month. The hardware store we used while building our home, gave us a 5% discount when we paid our entire bill before the 10th of the month.

When making multiple purchases, ask for an across the board discount. The worst they’ll say is “no”, but maybe they’ll say “yes.” Always ask.

Vehicle windshield replacement companies call offering to replace broken ones at a sale price. I would say, “No thanks, I don’t own a vehicle” and then hang up. If I had a broken windshield, I would call several companies to get estimates, and then make a decision about which company to go with.

Usually, brand name merchandise doesn’t mean a thing, except perhaps for our ego and high price. There are exceptions here. If we need to invest in a new tractor, lawnmower, things for work, or other purchases, which will be used for many years to come, then, naturally, go for the quality merchandise. But, compare. Perhaps the well-known expensive brand wouldn’t give the performance of a cheaper brand. Check prices, warrantees, and if it’s perfect for our needs. Do not buy to gloat over the label. Know how to differentiate these two reasons and act accordingly.

Large mouthed bottles and economy sized boxes: The bigger the bottle's mouth is, the faster the product pours out, hence, the more we use. I had been using small sample bottles of mouthwash. Then I bought a big bottle and what a surprise! No matter how careful I was, more came out into my mouth than ever before. So, using PAA, and my imagination, I used a funnel and poured from the big bottle back into the smaller empty ones. The giant economy size is still the cheapest way to go, and I'm not wasting mouthwash that pours out faster than the smaller container.

The same premise applies to laundry and dishwasher detergents. Buy the giant economy sizes, and pour the detergents into smaller containers. When it comes to handling heavier items, this works in our favor, as well.

Art and craft shows: Go the first day. Then go back an hour or so before closing on the last day. Some merchants would gladly discount a product for a sale, rather than spending time repacking it. Sometimes we can save money by haggling here, also.

Do we have an appliance or TV on the bum? Personally take it to a repair shop instead of calling a repairperson to our home. Home visits are expensive. Sometimes we need to mail the product for repair to a distant location. But always choose the cheapest way.

The suggestions in this chapter can be adapted to many other scenarios, as to fit any other circumstance in our life.

CHAPTER 22

UN-BUDGET

The last step in achieving financial astuteness is to have a life-long workable budget. This chapter explains the process.

We are sitting down, going over our monthly bills that are due now. AWCCK! The bills are much more than the money we have to pay them. Panic, stress, and perspiration explode our minds, giving us a headache from hell. Our brains are on fire; we want to scream this nightmare away. The month long buying rationalizations unleash their wrath. We, naively, thought our overspending would disappear. What has happened? What will we do? A few anxious moments pass and then we see it... A financial life preserver is being thrown to us. In the pocket is a copy of *A Life Preserver in a Sea of Debt*. We are saved!

The book teaches us the critical concept of positive attitude adjustment, which allows us to transition to financial stability, and it has essential lessons on budgeting our money. Pre-positive attitude adjustment fact: In the past we have tried diligently to set up a workable budget but most of our attempts ended in frustrating failures. This fact is dramatized by escalating personal debt. We need a workable alternative: a drastic change. Un-budget gives us this change.

Let's begin by eliminating the term "budget", which is a scary word, at best, and replace it with "un-budget." Its definition: Cut back on all expenditures, allowing the money saved to be used to cover all contingencies. It is a foolproof method, one that has worked for John throughout his life.

My scenario: As was mentioned in the first chapter, after my divorce in the late 1970s, my budgeting efforts were disastrous. There were always unexpected expenditures. Medical and dental bills, home maintenance, and vehicle repairs busted my budget. When insurance premiums came due, panic set in.

My three children still lived at home and we all felt the financial pinch. I reduced our food bills, cut back on buying clothes, and every other expense I could think of. I arranged to repay huge medical bills over three years in $5.00 and $10.00 increments. Even though it was hard, after each bill was paid in full, I reveled in my accomplishments and felt a sense of relief.

Though budgets may seem futile, they still have positive attributes. Budgets primarily show a list of fixed monthly expenses. They also show a secondary list of fluctuating expenses to prepare for before they are due, such as prescriptions to be filled. Using this old type budget list and practicing PAA assists us in evolving from budget to un-budget. When transition is complete we no longer need a written list because we have more than enough money to cover all expenses.

Add all sources of income, dividing in monthly amounts: salaries, income from stocks and other investments, capital gains, dividends, and interest. Then make an expenditure list:

1. Rent, mortgage, maintenance, expenditures, and fees
2. Utilities, including phone, electric, gas, and water
3. Clothing
4. Food, including snacks, restaurant bills, and take-out

5. Insurance, including life, house, and other
6. Taxes: legal and accountant fees
7. Credit card payments and other loans
8. Savings and retirement contributions. On payday, prearrange for direct deposits from our payroll account into savings and retirement accounts. Alter the amounts as necessary.
9. Transportation: gas, maintenance, parking, cab fare, subway and bus fare, freeway tolls, vehicle and bicycle upkeep and repairs, insurance, and registration
10. Household replacements and repairs, including appliances
11. Health and personal care (dues, personal hygiene, makeup, shaving needs, dry-cleaning, hair cuts, eye glasses and frames, doctors, dentists, and prescriptions, vitamins). John invested $20 for a hair clipper. I've cut his hair for five years. It's free!
12. Child care
13. Pocket money
14. Pets: Purchasing, veterinary bills, medications, food, toys, grooming, cages, leashes, etc.
15. Recreation: Sports, hobbies, toys, and lessons such as karate, dance, banjo, or other
16. Vacations
17. Charity contributions
18. Religious tithes and membership fees
19. Entertainment and gifts
20. Business expenses

21. Schools and tuition
22. Exterminators
23. Miscellaneous and emergency

We may need to add more categories depending on our lifestyle.

As we make our un-budget list, have separate columns for:

1. The amount we want to allocate for each item
2. The actual total for that particular expense
3. If the amount is more or less than our original estimate
4. Comments about how we can budget these items more effectively

Prorate bills and payments that come due quarterly, semi-annually, or yearly and include them in the list of monthly expenses.

This is our starting point. In reality mode, figure out if monthly income covers all expenses yet still leaves money to save. If not, put PAA in high gear, even if this means downsizing to a less expensive home or apartment. If we need to cut back to the bone in every conceivable way, we do it. If we need to work a second job, we do that, too. By consistently (and the word consistently is the key word), cutting back and doing with less, our finances even out.

Un-budget is a guideline, not a formula written in stone, nor is it anything to get fanatical about. At first, it may be easier to refer to our budget list, but the longer we use PAA the more we automatically know how to manage our money. If we cut back and save money wherever possible we have enough money to keep within our un-budget.

How far we cut back on spending is up to us, but the more we do cut back, the more money we will have in reserve. If cutting back is done in an apathetic manner, halfheartedly, nothing will be accomplished. Enjoy the cutbacks. We benefit. Feel good about it. Show a sense of humor; laugh in delight. Remember, we don't have to keep up with family, friends, or coworkers, and we have eliminated self-entitlements. Have fortitude to do what's best for us.

Everyone's lifestyle varies. Think about each un-budget item and how to reduce the cost. For example, cut grocery bills by purchasing less expensive meats, fish, and all other foods. Go shopping one less time a month and think of prices and health benefits of each item before purchasing. Avoid impulsive buying as it sabotages our goals. Eliminate or cut back junk foods. Always carry PAA with us while making un-budgeting a fun and challenging habit for all family members. Is everyone staying within it and are we stretching our dollars?

Keep in mind short-term and long-term goals. We are amazed at all the incidentals we can do without to reach those goals. Every cent not spent brings us closer to our financial goals and a balanced plus un-budget.

One common pitfall of managing old type budgets was overspending in *just one area* and then *just one more area.* This behavior deteriorated our budgets' foundation. Each month a different bill was left unpaid and late payment charges accrued. To succeed with un-budget, we cannot overspend in *just one area* and then *another area.*

I understand we all need to live a little, but not all the time. We can do what practically fits into our lifestyle and our un-budget. If we want to splurge, first, have the funds to back it up. And never splurge on a credit card. If there's no money for splurging, don't do it, or think of a free or inexpensive way. Do not think of it as an unpleasant sacrifice. Instead, think of it as transitioning to a debt-free life. Changes in our attitude lead to changes in our behavior. This sums up positive attitude adjustment. We win.

More un-budget tips:

1. Do maintenance on our progress and make changes where necessary.
2. Do not pay interest. Earn it with savings programs.
3. Keep rationalization and realization separate.

John succeeded with un-budget and he taught me how to succeed with it, as well. As this book has explained and demonstrated his un-budget secrets, we can follow suit and conquer our battles of overspending and debt. Stop living unconsciously: not being aware of the consequences of spending. Start living consciously while being aware of the consequences of spending. We can finally say goodbye to drowning in a sea of debt and say hello to our life preserver of positive attitude adjustment.

CONCLUSION

POSITIVE ATTITUDE ADJUSTED – TRIUMPHANT

Compliment us! We are committing ourselves to a permanent debt-free lifestyle. Thanks for investing time in this book. I know we will put the ideas and knowledge to the best possible use to help achieve our financial goals.

We can help ourselves retain the financial teachings of positive attitude adjustment by this quote from John F. Kennedy: "Peace is a daily, a weekly, a monthly process, gradually changing opinions, slowly eroding old barriers, quietly building new structures." Let us substitute financial astuteness for peace.

Here's a list of reminders:

1. Make positive attitude adjustment a permanent life preserver. Reach a happy medium. Do not cut back so far as to slip back into old habits.
2. Live a little. If some ideas are too severe, modify them. Any change is better than none at all. But over-modifying can defeat our purpose.
3. Be consistent and stay on course. Do not allow the attitudes of others or the great American marketing machine to sabotage our goals. If we slip, it's not a disaster. Pick up and try again.
4. Use impetus as our positive attitude motor to achieve financial fitness.
5. Keep this book as a review and research tool.

6. When an opportunity presents itself (PAA gives us the tools to make the transition from destructive spending to constructive financial astuteness), take advantage. Knowing that this critical information is available and not acting on it might bring years of regret later.
7. The more ideas we incorporate into our new everyday life style, the fewer old ways remain.
8. Some of us may be overwhelmed by so many new money saving ideas; we will give up before we begin. The trick is to start lowly. It is easier than plunging in all at once. Just take a few ideas at a time, become confident and comfortable with them, and then add more. Pretty soon we will have accomplished a debt-free life.
9. When deciding not to spend money where we did previously, do not spend the money on something else. Save it! Physically save it NOW – not later.
10. Nothing feels better than paying all our bills and having money left over.
11. Remember rationalization versus realization.
12. The first changes we make are the hardest. Each successive one becomes easier. Persevere. I did it. So can you.
13. If we want to save money, do not spend it. Say goodbye to impulse shopping.
14. If we must purchase a "need," get it at the cheapest available price or find it free. By being imaginative, we can

think of many more ways to save money.

15. Choose financial suggestions from this book that fit into our own individual lifestyles.
16. Have extra money? Do not reward our selves by buying anything. Celebrate, instead, with a special picnic in the park, even in winter, or other free activity.
17. John and I love to picnic in the winter in Glacier National Park (there is no entry fee in winter). This is a fun-filled recreation activity that includes snowball fights, hikes in deep snow, and building snowmen. One winter it started snowing and our sandwiches got soggy.
18. Positive attitude adjustment concepts are adaptable in other areas as well as finances. They can help us reach goals, make our dreams come true, and help us reach maximum health. PAA can be at the core of everything we do.
19. In the past we may have allowed ourselves to be pulled into the spending scenario. We saw government putting us into debt. We may have thought that credit card debt was the norm. We might have had the misconceived idea that it was our right to spend all earnings, and charge what our earnings did not cover. Now, positive attitude adjustment is our weapon against this "poisonous" financial thinking behavior. PAA is an ongoing mindset

throughout life. John and I are still discovering new ways to practice it.

20. We have learned to eliminate "it's only fifty cents or a dollar" purchases. We would rather see our hard earned money saved toward reaching future goals.
21. Eat it up, wear it out, and make it do, or do without.
22. Simplify and modify our lifestyles and have fun doing it. Avoid situations that culminate in needlessly spending money.
23. Instead of keeping up with the Jones's, keep up with our own savings agenda. Act not upon a self-indulgence, but rather act upon enhancing financial wellness.
24. Overspending perpetuates debt.
25. Knowing we have goals to reach, (adding to our emergency fund to have six months salary, or paying off medical and credit card bills), takes precedent over spending *anywhere*, even sale items.

Money: Respect it. Protect it. It will take care of us.

We are never too young or too old to start safeguarding our financial futures. Make a commitment that saving money and living debt-free will be our top priority. Then begin slowly to incorporate some of the easier suggestions in this book.

Eventually, our efforts will pay off and we will be excited to have more disposable income. The effect of PAA snowballs. Wear the PAA life preserver every day and watch the remarkable change that takes place in our lives as we go from worry and stress to tranquility and peace of mind.

Writing this book was one of the hardest challenges that I have ever faced. I had to struggle against the residuals of physical handicaps and brain injury as a result of having a stroke. But I kept pushing, and even when I had setbacks, I persisted until I finished. If I could manage to overcome my obstacles and finish *A Life Preserver in a Sea of Debt*, you can also accomplish the great feat of making a final transition to live within your means. It will take strength and fortitude, but you can do it!

Henry David Thoreau wrote in his book, *Walden*, "The mass of men lead lives of quiet desperation." Could these feelings drive people to go on spending sprees or to gamble away their life savings? Could it be the sensation that people experience when they spend more money than they make? Eradicate our desperation. Reach for the financial life preserver!

Having suffered a stroke when she was born, Judy was left with minor physical and mental handicaps. For 50 years she endured belittling and chastising from others, and had no self worth of her own. She grew up in south Florida, but has lived in Minnesota, New York, New Jersey, and Georgia. Judy has a close relationship with her three grown children. With the help of her second husband, John, she was able to overcome her past demons. They now live in northwest Montana, where they take pleasure in their organic garden and "put up" their own fruits and vegetables. Judy enjoys sewing, quilting, yard work, hiking, and visiting old ghost towns. The things that are most important to her are integrity, kindness, leading a healthy lifestyle, and a respect for the environment.

Lightning Source Inc.
LaVergne, TN USA
14 August 2009

154917LV00006B/57/P

9 781933 300160